MEXICO'S JUDICIAL STATISTICS.

ABSTRACT.

ANTONIO DE J. REMES DIAZ.

To my parents.

CONTENTS.

The numbers of this book represent Mexicans who are waiting for justice since long time ago…

SECOND EDITION MESSAGE.

More than 300 days have passed since MEXICO'S JUDICIAL STATISTICS: ABSTRACT first edition, and, certainly, this is consolidated as an unique text in Mexico and the rest of the world. Of course, our efforts have continued to disseminate the text as an independent book and I am pleased to know that there are convinced and surprised readers of its content.

Well, in this second edition, we have a follow-up regarding the strategic lines of investigation used in the predecessor work, through a process of monitoring and tracking judicial information from the Federal and States Courts, as well as the Attorney General's Offices, taking into account the original data and estimates of the first book in order to clarify the national judicial statistical process. This edition could be considered as a "*statistics compliance*" process, although this is a concept that, in my opinion, is too superfluous.

In any case, this book reiterates the contentious information pertaining to the Federal Government and the vast legal and contentious acquis generated before the Supreme Court of Justice of the Nation, the National Institute of Transparency, Access to Public Information and Data Protection (INAI) and its counterparts from the States, but now, confirming estimates, validating equations and methods, while increasing the initial repository, we have new sources of information and more databases. Of course, some details of style are made, as well as the presentation of the text in general.

An example of this confirmation is found thanks to the data of the 2019 National Census of State Justice Administration, where INEGI calculates RICLCRE of 26.90% (at least), while in the first edition of the work, the RICLCRE estimate at INEGI, 24.42% was foreseen, defining a margin of error of + -2.48% between both values, which supports the fidelity of the information and the forecasts used. Thanks to a method called "high card" (the highest data between those managed by INEGI and those investigated), in this second edition it can be confirmed, with a percentage higher than 97%, that the statistical information really exists in the country.

The spirit of our work continues in the universe of the revelation of the vicissitudes and general problems of the Justice Administration at present regarding the judicial statistics they produce and with which it accounts to society, highlighting that in the country there are pre-existing pending cases with more than 50 years.

Similarly, this work continues to reveal a summary of timely judicial information, unpublished discoveries about the courts from Mexico objectivily, statistical and graphic clarifications, as well as a "*sabermetrics*" approach to Mexico's courts, fairly pondering as an indispensable public service to more than 125 million people.

On the other hand, I consider interesting to mention a rational belief that I have regarding the impact that this work will have at some moment between the lawyers: *to motivate a Judicial Reform that truly serves Mexicans.*

In October 2019, the political class of the Mexican legal forum headed by the Minister President of the Supreme Court of Justice Arturo Zaldivar Lelo de Larrea, the Legal Counsel of the Federal Government Julio Scherer Ibarra and the Senator Ricardo Monreal Ávila, met in the former building of the Senate of the Republic with the purpose of drawing a critical route of "*judicial reform*". Of course, the "spirit" of improving social misperception, more like an "institutional purge" of one of the State Branches, justifies its initiative.

Notwithstanding the foregoing, the President of Mexico, Andres Manuel Lopez Obrador, has stated that: "*I am not in favor of taking a Constitutional reform initiative to renew the Judicial Power from the outside, this was done when President Zedillo. I am not going to proceed in this way, I am not going to send any initiative or because we have the majority of legislators, we are not going to act in that way, because I consider that the best renewal must arise within the Judiciary* (Press conference, September 5, 2019).

Likewise, President Lopez Obrador says: "*I think that the reform of the Judiciary has to take place within the same Judiciary, that the Judiciary has to reform itself and there is the possibility of achieving it with the renewed Judiciary and also with the Supreme Court of Justice of the Nation and in particular with the president of the Supreme Court of Justice of the Nation, which is a straight, complete Justice*"; "*As an independent branch, they can carry out the changes that the Judiciary needs, because, without a doubt, there is corruption in the Judiciary* (Press conference,October 22, 2019)."

For these reasons, if there is a judicial reform, such as the one that "moves" in that subtle world of politics, we are faced with a purely cosmetic (malarkey) initiative that fails to address the causes of the country's institutional problem.

Finally, my interest in continuing with these statistical analyzes at the national level will be reduced to this second edition, since certainly, in the country, there are Authorities such as State Units and informants of the System, who receive both federal budgets and remuneration for doing statistical information work. Therefore, it is not possible that with all the State infrastructure, these people do not do their job and cannot give the official information. **It is a truly disappointing**!

Regardless of that belief, as I propose, it will be until the Spring of 2025, when I dare to carry out, in any case, a different statistical exercise of the same caliber, to confirm the weighted numbers, at least that of the destination, as in baseball, we have a significant surprise, likewise the bottom of the ninth inning.

Baby Shark, dududu, baby shark…

January 2020.

I.   Introduction.

This essay has the essential purpose of revealing the situation of the Justice Administration in Mexico through two strategic research guidelines:

ONE, to disclose the status of pending legal cases in Federal Courts, State Courts, Labor, and Bureaucratic Labor Courts, under three time periods: 1) legal proceedings before December 31, 1999; 2) legal matters between January 1, 2000 to December 31, 2010 and 3) legal cases from January 2011 to date; and

TWO, to reveal the situation of legal cases disputed by Federal Government represented by the Legal Counsel of the President of Mexico, Legal Units and lawyers, in the period from January 1, 2000, to January 23, 2019, and to inform the pending legal cases.

The book starts with a brief introduction regarding the legal and technical bases of Judicial Statistics in Mexico and summarizes the available data coming from the National Census of Justice Administration and the Criminal Prosecution in Federal and states Jurisdiction, produced by the National Institute of Statistics and Geography (INEGI), as the statistics provided by Administrative, Labor and Bureaucratic Labor Courts. From each of the available sources, these details are specified, and some problems are detected.

Moreover, the abstract informs an almanac of legal information of 180 answers to Public Information Petitions processed in the National Transparency Platform (PNT) of the National Institute of Transparency, Access to Information and Personal Data Protection, (INAI), and the *grandfathered* INFOMEX Transparency Federal Government and states software.

It is essential to say that the research focuses on 200 authorities and Courts coming from the 32 states of Mexico and the Federal Government, including the Attorney General of the Republic and the 32 states Attorney General, trying to undertake all the pending cases in Constitutional Law, Civil Law, Commercial Law, Family Law, Criminal Law, Administrative Law, Labor Law, Bureaucratic Labor Law, Agrarian Law, International Public Law, International Private Law and Military Law.

Furthermore, the essay reveals the legal disputations before Transparency Regulators in Federal and State Jurisdictions, because of the lack of public information that corroborates Public Accountability.

Also, this paper informs the Constitutional Controversy case 214/2018 (correlated to cases 9/2019 and 117/2018) before the Supreme Court of Justice of the Nation *INEGI v. INAI*. The Constitutional Controversy case 214/2018 is caused by the favorable resolution of the claim RRA 6844/19 before INAI *(where the author is the petitioner)* forcing to INEGI to reveal public information and legal statistics regarding the Average Duration of Resolution of Legal Cases (*ADRLC*) in Federal and states Jurisdictions.

Despite the result of the Constitutional Case 214/2018, this abstract reveals the vicissitudes and the general problems of the Justice Administration regarding the Judicial Statistics produced by courts for Public Accountability. Similarly, this text highlights the existence of pending cases with more than 50 years of legal disputation.

Finally, it is essential to mention that this abstract has been written thanks to Public Information collected, by the Fundamental Right to Access to Public Information and Public Accountability, article 6, section A, of the Political Constitution of the United States of Mexico.

Generally, the book reveals a summary of timely Judicial Information, unpublished discoveries about the Legal System throughout the country with an objective point of view; statistical and graphical precisions, as well as a *sabermetric* approach to the Justice Administration, pondering fairly the institutions that, equally, provide an essential public service to 107 million people.

Spring of 2019.

II. Judicial Statistics Bases, available information, and precisions.

Mexico's Judicial Statistics are public information produced by the Public Treasury, according to article 6, section A, clause I, of the Political Constitution of United States of Mexico, articles 3, clause VII and 70, clause XXX, of the Transparency and Access to Public Information General Act[1]. Judicial Statistics allow knowing the actual performance of the Justice Administration executing functions, faculties, and competencies to the highest degree of possible disaggregation.

On the other side, article 26, section B, of the Political Constitution of the United States of Mexico, establishes that Mexico will have a National System of Statistics and Geography whose data will be considered official. The autonomous constitutional regulator in statistics is the National Institute of Statistics and Geography (INEGI), a Public Institution that has vast data sources integrated after 36 years, infrastructure, human resources and a Federal Budget of $12,129,702,814.00.

Besides, the National System of Statistical Information and Geography Act, according to article 2, clause XV, establishes as a State Unit the Bureau who has attributions to develop statistical and geographical activities, as well as administrative records capable of obtaining National Interest Information from:

a) Federal Government Authorities, including the President of Mexico and the Attorney General of the Republic;

b) Legislative Branch, and Judicial Branch;

c) States and Municipalities, including Mexico City;

---

[1] POLITICAL CONSTITUTION OF THE UNITED STATES OF MEXICO Article 6. "...The right to information shall be guaranteed by the State. ...... I. All information in possession of any authority, entity, body and agency of the Executive, Legislative and Judicial Powers, autonomous bodies, political parties, trusts and public funds, as well as any individual, moral or union that receives and exercises public resources or perform acts of authority at the federal, state and municipal levels, it is public and may only be temporarily reserved for reasons of public interest and national security, in the terms established by law. In the interpretation of this right, the principle of maximum publicity must prevail. The obligated subjects must document any act that derives from the exercise of their faculties, powers or functions, the law will determine the specific cases under which the declaration of non-existence of the information will proceed.

d) Autonomous Constitutional Regulators and

e) Administrative Federal Courts.

According to article 28 Bis of the National System of Statistical Information and Geography Act, there is a National Sub-System of Government, Public Safety and Justice Administration that will have as a goal to institutionalize and to operate a coordinated scheme for the production, integration, conservation and dissemination of statistical and geographic National Interest Information, of quality, pertinence, truth and timeliness that allows to know the situation that the management and the performance of the institutions keep public that make up the State and its respective powers in the functions of Government, Public Safety, and Justice, to support the processes of design, implementation, monitoring, and evaluation of public policies in these matters.

It should be noted that the National Sub-System of Government, Public Safety and Justice Administration was created by Directive 4a/X/2008 of the Government Board of INEGI in 2008. Since then, its duty has been relevant through the implementation of the National Census of Federal and the State Justice Administration, and collaborating with the State Supreme Courts, noticing the National Net of Judicial Statistics of the National Commission of Supreme Courts of Justice of the States of Mexico (CONATRIB)[2].

In other words, according to the National Transparency System, regarding to Judicial Statistics, there are two legal bases correlated to produce, to integrate and to spread as public information: the foundation as a State Unit coming from an Obligated Authority coordinated by INEGI and the basis of public information that every Obligated Authority must produce rendering its competencies, faculties, and functions.

Without pretending to dismiss the institutional efforts aimed at improving the Justice Administration, nowadays it is crucial to say that in Mexico, the availability of disaggregated Judicial Statistics with indicators of the Court Functions in Federal

---

[2] See in http://conatrib.org.mx/rejconatrib/

and State jurisdictions that reveal the information of Public Interest and National Concern, in a detailed, uniform, transparent and intelligible structure; it has deficiency in technical and fundamentals standards that avoid elucidating the objective performance rendering its competencies, faculties and functions financed by Public Treasury, and to provide Public Accountability.

As a matter of interest, it is essential to say that, in the petition 4010000011519 by grandfathered INFOMEX Federal Government software, INEGI was asked to reveal what agreements had celebrated with Federal Courts, Administrative Federal Courts, Labor, and Bureaucratic Labor Courts and State Courts, in each of the 32 states of Mexico, in order to coordinate, to produce, to integrate, to preserve and to disseminate Judicial Statistics, from January 25, 1983, to date.

INEGI answered as follows:

"... an exhaustive search was carried out in the different Administrative Units that could have required information, in this regard we inform you the following:

About to the Directorate General of Socio-demographic Statistics, it is specified that the statistics on labor relations of local jurisdiction are generated with an annual periodicity and are available for the period from 1991 to 2017, they have as an informant source the Local Conciliation Boards and Arbitration in each of the states. It should be mentioned that the General Directorate of Sociodemographic Statistics has not signed an agreement with the Local Conciliation and Arbitration Boards.

Notwithstanding the above, in the Regional Offices and State Coordinations of the

Institute it is reported that INEGI has signed three agreements as follows:

...

...

The conceptual framework that functions as a technical scheme for the creation of statistics generated from the information provided by the Local Conciliation and Arbitration Boards can be consulted in the Methodological Summary of labor relations statistics of local jurisdiction, available in the INEGI website:

https://www.inegi.org.mx/app/biblioteca/ficha.html?upc=702825091026

As well as the Technical Standard for the National Classification of Crimes for Statistical Purposes, a document that is available for public consultation at the following electronic address:

https://www.dof.gob.mx/nota_detalle.php?codigo=5541706&fecha=22/10/2018

On the part of the General Directorate of Government, Public Security and Justice Statistics, particularly the Deputy General Directorate of Government Information Policies and National Government Censuses, states that since 2009 (the year in which the Deputy General Directorate of Information of Government, Public Security and Impartition of Justice) to date, there is no agreement with the Judicial Branch of the Federation, the Federal Administrative Court, the Higher Agrarian Court, the Federal Board of Conciliation and Arbitration, the Supreme Court of Justice of the 32 states of Mexico and its Judiciary Councils, the Boards of Conciliation and Arbitration and the Bureaucratic Courts of the States, as well as the States Administrative Courts,. The work on statistics is coordinated through the Specialized Technical Committee on Justice Information. Likewise, there is general agreement number 015/2014 by which the National Commission of Superior Courts of Justice (CONATRIB) undertakes to consolidate strategic statistical projects for the delivery of justice with INEGI. It is attached for quick reference. (Annex 4)

Likewise, it is reported that in the Conceptual Frameworks corresponding to each of the information programs up to now developed in the field of justice delivery at the state and federal levels, and you will be able to identify the topics of your interest, which can be consulted in the following websites:

States:

- CNIJE 2018:
http://www.beta.inegi.org.mx/app/biblioteca/ficha.html?upc=702825104429

- CNIJE 2017:
http://www.beta.inegi.org.mx/app/biblioteca/ficha.html?upc=702825095437

- CNIJE 2016:
http://www.beta.inegi.org.mx/app/biblioteca/ficha.html?upc=702825088644

- CNIJE 2015:

*http://www.beta.inegi.org.mx/app/bibliote
ca/ficha.html?upc=702825078263*

- CNIJE 2014:

*http://www.beta.inegi.org.mx/app/bibliote
ca/ficha.html?upc=702825064587*

Federal:

- CNIJF 2018:

*http://www.beta.inegi.org.mx/app/bibliote
ca/ficha.html?upc=702825101961*

- CNIJF 2017:

*http://www.beta.inegi.org.mx/app/bibliote
ca/ficha.html?upc=702825094027*

- CNIJF 2016:

*http://www.beta.inegi.org.mx/app/bibliote
ca/ficha.html?upc=702825088620*

- CNIJF 2015:

*http://www.beta.inegi.org.mx/app/bibliote
ca/ficha.html?upc=702825080785*

- CNIJF 2014:

*http://www.beta.inegi.org.mx/app/bibliote
ca/ficha.html?upc=702825074067".*

Regarding the previous transcript, regardless of the revealed bases of the statistical projects carried out by INEGI, it can be concluded that in Mexico, the production of judicial statistics lacks technical and legal bases in order to work uniformly and consolidated as an instrument of Public Accountability, according to functions, faculties, and competencies of the Justice Administration.

Exposed the bases of the Judicial Statistics, next to diverse data coming from governmental beings are presented using of a brief analysis of the available public information and legal records of Federal Courts, as a prospective starting point.

1. National Institute of Statistics and Geography (INEGI).

National Census of State Justice Administration 2017[3]. 80,166,627 petitions and services at State Courts in 2016; 2.7 % represent plaintiffs, complaints, exhortations and motions; that said 2,164,499 cases.

There were 1´753,653 cases at the beginning, received 1´932,535, and 1´402,932 concluded (38.05%), pending 1´838,766[4], that is, 57,462 legal cases approximately in each of the 32 states of Mexico.

According to National Disaggregation, 40.2% are Family Law, 32.2% Civil Law; 20.1% Business Law, 5.9% Criminal Law; 1.3% other and .3% Teenage Law.

In the beginning, there were 108,405 Criminal Law cases, received 118,817, and 155,343 concluded, pending 151,060; noticing 45% Traditional Criminal Justice System and 55% New Criminal Justice System.

National Census of State Justice Administration 2018[5]. 38,366,724 petitions and services at State Courts in 2017; 7.1% represent plaintiffs, complaints, exhortations and motions (2´724,037 cases).

Received 2´008,661 cases, 1´317,371 concluded (65.58%) pending 2´320,248[6] cases, that is, 72,508 files approximately at each of the 32 states of Mexico.

According to National Disaggregation, 40.6% are Family Law; 30.2% Civil Law, 20.9% Business Law, 6.9% Criminal Law, 1.1% other and 0.3% Teenage Law. 74.1% were Traditional System and 23.3% New System.

---

[3] General Results, available in https://inegi.org.mx/programas/cnije/2017/
[4] Official records of the National Census were updated after the General Results by INEGI.
[5] General Results, available in https://inegi.org.mx/programas/cnije/2018/
[6] *Idem, Op cit 5.*

There were 144,741 Criminal Law cases, 114,425 resolutions and 222,553 pending, with disaggregation of 87.4% New Criminal Justice System and 12.6% Traditional Criminal Justice System.

National Census of State Justice Administration 2019. 31 million 003 thousand 807 procedures and services; of that total, 2 million 126 thousand 005 judicial records, including criminal cases[7].

1,191,517 files were entered and 1,153,542 were completed, with a total of 3,066,386 pending cases[8]. Of that disaggregated, 41.7% is family matter, 32.2% civil matter, 24. 5% commercial matter and 1.6% other matter.

In criminal cases, 172,718 cases entered, 106, 707 were resolved and 269,875 cases were pending, disaggregating 93.3% of criminal cases under the New Criminal Justice System and 6.6% of the Elder one.

1.1. Precisions.

- The National Census of State Justice Administration made by INEGI represents the first evidence of objective data regarding the implementation of Criminal Law and Human Rights constitutional reforms in the states of Mexico. The National Census is the analytical instrument with more uniformity of the whole Judicial Statistics.

- According to the National Census of State Justice Administration 2018, at the end of 2017, there were these pending legal cases:

Justice Administration (Except Criminal Law) pending cases.					
Total					
	TOTAL	Civil Law	Business Law	Family Law	Other
MEXICO	**2,097,695**	756,182	412,064	917,889	11,560

---

[7] RESULTADOS GENERALES, Censo Nacional de Impartición de Justicia Estatal 2019, available in https://www.inegi.org.mx/programas/cnije/2019/
[8] Idem.

Aguascalientes	133,804	26,149	63,936	43,719	0
Baja California	155,150	89,931	23,666	41,553	
Campeche	8,126	3,077	1,690	3,359	0
Coahuila de Zaragoza	85,676	22,242	33,588	29,846	
Colima	0				0
Chiapas	86,294	11,966	23,521	50,807	
Mexico City	396,310	178,336		217,974	
Durango	33,116	7,366	9,064	16,686	
Guanajuato	65,600	16,286	41,865	7,449	
Guerrero	103,316	17,305	29,678	56,333	
Hidalgo	95,439	36,182	14,330	44,927	
Jalisco	0	0	0	0	
State of Mexico	74,000	16,162	19,123	38,715	
Michoacan de Ocampo	58,263	36,086	4,117	18,060	0
Morelos	75,944	37,207	0	38,737	
Nayarit	27,694	5,190	8,109	14,395	
Nuevo Leon	57,216	11,499	9,430	26,744	9,543
Oaxaca	105,786	6,090	18,146	81,550	
Puebla	61,785	17,919	10,660	31,189	2,017
Queretaro	44,610	9,244	21,246	14,120	
Quintana Roo	15,004	5,430	1,831	7,743	
San Luis Potosi	5,826	967	910	3,949	
Sinaloa	53	53			
Sonora	41,160	6,632	19,076	15,452	
Tabasco	32,332	32,266	66	0	
Tamaulipas	31,705	5,818	4,917	20,970	
Tlaxcala	38,749	13,323	4,202	21,224	
Veracruz de Ignacio de la Llave	205,673	123,056	31,518	51,099	
Yucatan	25,723	6,284	6,763	12,676	
Zacatecas	33,341	14,116	10,612	8,613	
Source: INEGI. National Census of State Justice Administration 2018.					

- According to the National Census of State Justice Administration 2018 data, at the end of 2017, there were these Criminal Law pending cases:

Criminal Law in the states of Mexico
Considering System, Phase and Court.
2017

Jurisdiction	Pending		
	TCJS	NCJS	
		Court	Tribunal
MEXICO	71 491	129 922	16 794
Aguascalientes	219	1 049	6
Baja California	8 514	8 663	135
Baja California Sur	1 411	535	1
Campeche	1 897	565	3
Coahuila de Zaragoza	1 058	5 494	0
Colima	0	-	-
Chiapas	1 369	1 545	11
Chihuahua	-	-	-
Mexico City	11 984	5 653	175
Durango	1 121	6 732	42
Guanajuato	2 497	12 448	82
Guerrero	7 067	1 003	25
Hidalgo	562	1 487	1
Jalisco	10 531	4 635	1
State of Mexico	-	42 739	15 156
Michoacan de Ocampo	1 332	2 857	193
Morelos	0	873	56
Nayarit	2 246	1 212	4
Nuevo Leon	73	3 989	556
Oaxaca	1 117	3 212	188
Puebla	3 143	4 293	5
Queretaro	287	1 650	23
Quintana Roo	426	885	4
San Luis Potosi	-	1 506	26

Sinaloa	93	1 338	18
Sonora	446	3 020	0
Tabasco	7 720	4 898	2
Tamaulipas	211	1 303	33
Tlaxcala	2 887	195	1
Veracruz de Ignacio de la Llave	1 293	1 879	43
Yucatan	348	592	3
Zacatecas	1 639	3 672	1

- INEGI's pending cases were uploaded in March 9, 2018, and there is an arithmetic variation of the official numbers despite the 1, 402,932 resolutions, at the beginning there were 1´753,653 and 1´932,535 are received in 2016, so there are **2´283,256 pending cases at the end of 2016** (*Legal cases existing 2016 plus Legal cases received 2016 minus legal cases concluded 2016*) not the revealed data, 1´838,766 pending cases, that represent **444,490 cases as an error range.**

- In another aspect, according to National Census of State Justice Administration 2018 uploaded at January 31, 2019; regarding the situation of received during 2017 of Civil Law, Family Law and Commercial Law, without Criminal Law legal cases, there are 1´898,651[9] files, while the official data exposes 1´863,920, having a difference of 34,731 cases, that said, 1.83% range of difference between legal proceedings reported and legal cases revealed.

- **The Real Institutional Capacity of Legal Case Resolution (RICLCRE)[10]** of State Courts calculated in the National Census of State Justice Administration 2017 is 38.05% (*concluded cases / received cases + pending cases*) and 2018 RICLCRE was 30.69% (*Concluded cases / received cases +pending cases*), pending **2´974,546 legal cases at State Courts, estimating 92,955 files per each of the 32 states of Mexico.**

---

[9] Available in
https://www.inegi.org.mx/sistemas/olap/consulta/general_ver4/MDXQueryDatos.asp?proy=
[10] REAL INSTITUTIONAL CAPACITY OF LEGAL CASE RESOLUTION (RICLCRE) Full concept available in Chapter V, *Legal sabermetric discoveries: prospective*; question b.

That means, despite the legal and constitutional implementation of the New Legal System, RICLCRE was *reduced* **19.34% regarding received and pending cases in 2016 and 2017.**

As a matter of interest, it is known that INEGI has already revealed the National Census of Impartition of State Justice 2019 where it handles the most up-to-date data[11].

- Prior to its deliberation and according to the data collected from the 2017 and 2018 censuses, a percentage of income of + 3.8% (income 2016 / income 2017) could be estimated at the figure of the previous year and a percentage of matters resolved from - 6.1% (matters concluded 2016 / matters concluded 2017) to the figure of the year 2017. According to this estimate base, in 2018, it was calculated at first that, in the State Courts, 2,084,990 cases entered and 1, 237,011 were resolved, providing as RICLCRE of 24.42% effectiveness (cases concluded 2018 / cases entered 2018+ issues lagging 2017) and pending cases during 2018 of 3, 827,525 claims.

Now, according to the data of the Official Census, we have the following variations of data:

DATA	ESTIMATE 2018	CENSUS 2019	VARIATION	REAL ESTIMATE
ENTRIES	2, 084,990 (+3.8%)	1,961,517	-1.36%	2.44% (+)
CONCLUDED	1,237,011 (-6.1%)	1,153,542	+0.59%	5.51% (-)
PENDING	3,827,525	3,066,386	+19.89%	**3,782,521**
RICLCRE	24.42%	26.90%	-2.48%	**23.36%**

---

[11] According to the information available at https://www.snieg.mx/#4 in the National Interest Information calendar, it is reported that the 2019 National Censuses took on July 5, 2019 the National Census of Federal Justice Administration 2019 and on October 25 the National Census of State Justice Administration 2019.

Due to the values shown in 2016, 2017 and 2018 as RICLCRE (38.05 and 30.69 and 23.36%), it is confirmed that the effectiveness of the State Courts was reduced by 2018 by 23.89% compared to previous year; and from the period from 2016 to 2018, in three years, 38.61%, being in that case that disability value of the State similar to the one initially calculated at the beginning of the Criminal Reform, in budgetary and state infrastructure terms.

RICLCRE REDUCTION 2016 to 2018		
ESTIMATE	REAL	DIFFERENCE
20.43% (Fiscal year)	23.89% (fiscal year)	+3.46%
35.82% (consolitaded)	38.61% (consolitaded)	+2.79%

- Also, in Criminal Law cases, regarding the National Census of State Justice Prosecution 2018[12], there were **1,197,732 pending cases, noticing 167,853 files of Criminal Investigations of the TCJS:**

CRIMINAL PROSECUTION			
	TOTAL	CRIMINAL PROSECUTION TCJS	CRIMINAL PROSECUTION NCJS
MEXICO	**1,197,732**	**167,853**	**1,029,879**
Aguascalientes	9,639	0	9,639
Baja California	69,913	0	69,913
Campeche	909	0	909
Coahuila de Zaragoza	61,387	5,196	56,191
Colima	15,268	0	15,268
Chiapas	21,949	21	21,928
Chihuahua	56,634	0	56,634
Mexico City	28,367	0	28,367

---

[12] Available in https://inegi.org.mx/programas/cnpje/2018/

Durango	23,705	0	23,705
Guanajuato	63,117	5	63,112
Guerrero	22,997	1,851	21,146
Hidalgo	139,214	75,263	63,951
Jalisco	128,971	31,517	97,454
State of Mexico	114,222	0	114,222
Michoacan de Ocampo	20,053	9	20,044
Morelos	32	0	32
Nayarit	497	0	497
Nuevo Leon	57,779	8	57,771
Oaxaca	21,305		21,305
Puebla	38,773	7,225	31,548
Queretaro	36,875	23	36,852
Quintana Roo	10,124	4,374	5,750
San Luis Potosi	18,860	0	18,860
Sinaloa	59,672	34,130	25,542
Tabasco	41,109	0	41,109
Tamaulipas	28,334	0	28,334
Tlaxcala	5,549	0	5,549
Veracruz de Ignacio de la Llave	50,729	643	50,086
Yucatan	38,870	7,578	31,292
Zacatecas	12,879	10	12,869
SOURCE: INEGI. National Census of State Justice Prosecution 2018.			

Then, in the National Census of State Justice Prosecution 2019, there are the following investigations pending:

CRIMINAL PROSECUTION 2018

STATE	PENDING

	CRIMINAL PROSECUTION TCJS	CRIMINAL PROSECUTION NCJS
MEXICO	**280 448**	**1 260 234**
Aguascalientes	18 979	32 604
Baja California	0	72 823
Baja California Sur	72	30 968
Campeche	-	1 086
Coahuila de Zaragoza	-	41 126
Colima	45	33 374
Chiapas	0	9 655
Chihuahua	0	58 697
Mexico City	12 575	135 352
Durango	0	19 929
Guanajuato	2	74 941
Guerrero	53 130	26 567
Hidalgo	26 155	78 522
Jalisco	2 037	125 826
México	0	134 243
Michoacan de Ocampo	0	19 488
Morelos	0	33 618
Nayarit	27	2 224
Nuevo Leon	6	57 524
Oaxaca	12 179	32 048
Puebla	15 646	80 797
Querétaro	9	40 746
Quintana Roo	47 664	25 509
San Luis Potosi	0	22 900
Sinaloa	ND	ND
Sonora	533	-
Tabasco	-	33 761
Tamaulipas	0	-
Tlaxcala	0	8 749
Veracruz de Ignacio de la Llave	75	-
Yucatán	91 065	11 561

Zacatecas	249	15 596
SOURCE: INEGI. National Census of State Justice Prosecution 2019.		

The previous comparison of disaggregated data is certainly important from a statistical point of view since the beginning of the validity of the New Criminal Justice System, in 2018, there are at least 280,448 previous inquiries pending to be recorded, which is far from of the statistical control of the State Prosecutors that calculated in 2017 at 167,853, that is, more than 112,595 records of the previous system that appeared in the prosecutors.

One example of these issues related to the power report of the informants of the system we have in Mexico City. For example, the Attorney General of Mexico City reported in 2017 28,367 investigation files as pending, but 365 days later, it manifests 135,352 cases and 12,575 of TCJS, that is, 147,927 pending files, an increase of 521.47% regarding its statistical control.

- Moreover, the National Census of Federal Justice Prosecution 2018[13], closing 2017 there were 17,986 Criminal Prosecutions TCJS and 36,380 NCJS pending; also 24,381 Criminal Prosecutions TCJS and 23,539 NCJS reassigned. Furthermore, in closing 2017, 13,247 arrest warrants were pending.

2. General Bureau of Judicial Statistics of the Federal Judiciary Council (CJF)

In 2017[14], the Federal Judiciary Council reported 1´089, 591 received cases in all the Federal District and Circuit Courts, where 1´079,247 cases were concluded, pending 334,777. CJF informed that the RICLCRE was 99.05%.

Then, in 2018[15], CJF reveals 1´104,180 received cases and 1´107,008 concluded cases, pending 332,105, with 100% RICLCRE.

2.1. Precisions.

---

[13] Available in https://inegi.org.mx/programas/cnpj/2018/
[14] Avaialble in ANEXO ESTADÍSTICO 2017, https://www.dgepj.cjf.gob.mx/resources/anexos/2017/graficas/PAN_NAL_TOT_17.pdf
[15] Available in ANEXO ESTADÍSTICO 2018, https://www.dgepj.cjf.gob.mx/resources/anexos/2018/graficas/PAN_NAL_TOT_18.pdf

- According to CJF's RICLCRE, it is essential to say that INEGI has calculated in the National Census of Federal Justice Administration 2017 and 2018[16] 78.4% during 2017 and 78.3% in 2016, disagreeing 21.3% RICLCRE variation.

- Comparing the data, CJF's RICLCRE 2017 is 74.20% (*concluded cases 2017/ pending cases 2016 + received cases 2017*) and 2018 RICLCRE is 75.00% *(concluded cases 2018/ pending cases 2017+ received cases 2017),* increasing +1.01% effectiveness.

- To this day, it is convenient to say that the Judicial Branch of the Federation is the only Court in the country that has a succinctly disaggregated analysis of the average duration of resolution of its affairs according to the National Census of Federal Justice Administration 2018 and 2019.

The calendar days that have been disaggregated thanks to the National Census of Impartition of Federal Justice 2018 and 2019 of INEGI are the following:

Proceeding	ADRLC 2017	ADRLC 2018	Difference (+/-)
Criminal case	539	529	-10
Constitutional class action	299	**590**	+291
Civil and Administrative	280	276	-4
Amparo Direct Trial appeal	234	206	-28
Commercial trial	179	**205**	+26
Amparo trial before Circuit Court	167	163	-4
Amparo appeal	156	**157**	+1
Appeals before SCJN	100	**116**	+16
Amparo trial before District Court	96	94	-2
Claims	57	57	=
number of days			

---

[16] Available in http://www.beta.inegi.org.mx/programas/cnijf/2013/

- Now, in Bank of Mexico (BANXICO) research *Eficiencia del Sistema de Justicia y Desempeño Económico Regional en México (2017)[17]"* there is a national estimate disaggregated by days of Commercial Law disputations in the 32 states of Mexico:

Anexo

Tabla A1. Estadísticos Descriptivos de las Variables Empleadas

	Tiempo de resolución de Disputas (número de días)					Crecimiento Económico[1]	Índice de Infraestructura[2]	Fraccionalización Etnolingüística
	2007	2009	2012	2014	Promedio			
Aguascalientes	290	327	271	305	298	1.78	1.70	0.45
Baja California	470	446	416	416	437	-0.89	0.90	2.81
Baja California Sur	581	497	497	525	525	-0.43	0.60	3.61
Campeche	430	361	355	280	357	-1.23	0.20	21.59
Coahuila	422	270	270	270	308	1.22	0.90	0.49
Colima	245	343	310	310	302	0.65	2.90	1.34
Chiapas	386	386	337	337	362	0.15	-0.80	45.01
Chihuahua	280	290	290	290	288	0.61	0.60	6.82
Distrito Federal	345	415	415	400	394	2.28	3.50	2.95
Durango	306	259	243	228	259	0.54	0.20	4.28
Guanajuato	326	385	385	288	346	1.92	0.90	0.59
Guerrero	304	375	375	375	357	0.54	-0.90	27.46
Hidalgo	280	330	320	320	313	0.75	0.50	26.25
Jalisco	275	360	360	360	339	0.85	1.10	1.56
México	318	375	375	350	355	0.83	1.60	6.75
Michoacán	381	390	340	340	363	0.95	0.40	3.79
Morelos	390	461	461	461	443	1.15	1.80	5.27
Nayarit	429	310	310	310	340	0.24	0.60	10.04
Nuevo León	320	236	236	236	262	1.53	1.40	1.85
Oaxaca	330	300	353	353	334	1.23	-1.00	54.01
Puebla	445	391	391	372	400	0.96	0.50	20.87
Querétaro	290	324	324	324	316	2.43	1.10	3.49
Quintana Roo	568	560	560	375	516	0.72	0.60	27.63
San Luis Potosí	360	381	341	341	356	1.62	0.10	19.58
Sinaloa	337	290	290	270	297	0.79	0.80	1.82
Sonora	372	366	366	366	368	1.81	0.70	4.83
Tabasco	353	314	314	314	324	1.15	0.40	5.76
Tamaulipas	415	301	245	245	302	-0.04	0.80	1.56
Tlaxcala	415	484	455	455	452	0.26	1.90	4.99
Veracruz	470	382	470	435	439	0.96	0.10	17.37
Yucatán	495	428	398	498	455	0.84	0.50	41.89
Zacatecas	230	248	248	248	244	3.07	0.40	0.74
Promedio	371	363	354	344	358	0.91	0.78	11.80
Desviación estándar	86.6	74.2	78.4	74.9	70.5	0.90	0.94	14.40
Mínimo	230	248	236	228	244	-1.23	-1.00	0.45
Máximo	581	560	560	525	525	3.07	3.50	54.01

1/ Tasa de crecimiento promedio anual del PIB per cápita excluyendo la actividad petrolera.
2/ El índice se presenta en forma estandarizada y se obtuvo de Chávez y López (2013).
Fuente: Banco Mundial (reporte *Doing Business*, varios años) y estimaciones propias con datos de INEGI y del reporte *Doing Business* del Banco Mundial.

---

[17] BANXICO; *Eficiencia del Sistema de Justicia y Desempeño Económico Regional en México.* Written by Juan Carlos Chavez Martín del Campo, Felipe J. Fonseca and Manuel de J. Gómez Zaldivar. June 2017, available in http://www.anterior.banxico.org.mx/publicaciones-y-discursos/publicaciones/documentos-de-investigacion/banxico/%7B172DEC87-7CAB-3592-A8A5-1EA2F879DC1F%7D.pdf; page 14.

3. Bureau of Statistics of the Higher Agrarian Court.

In the period from July 21, 1992, to June 30, 2018, the Bureau of Statistics of the Higher Agrarian Court[18] reveals a consolidated abstract of 984,726 received cases and 934,826 concluded cases, pending 49,900 files (5.07%).

3.1. Precisions.

- Agrarian Judicial Statistics are not disaggregated despite the existence of the Bureau of Statistics faculty to undertake that duty[19].

4. Bureau of General Administration of the Federal Bureaucratic Labor Court.

According to its consolidated judicial statistics, in the period between 1995 and 2018 (deadline December 31th 2018), there are 26,339 active cases, where 15,088 have not a resolution, 57.28%.

It is essential to say that statistical records demonstrate 20 cases from 1995 to 2000 pending; 824 cases from 2001 to 2007 in the same situation; 3,552 from 2008 to 2014, and 10,692 pending cases from 2015 to deadline 2018.

4.1. Precisions.

- There are 3,000 pending cases at least with one waiting decade of judicial resolution.

- Considering 15,088 cases without resolution and the previous periods, in 2018 there were 4,365 received cases and 38 concluded cases, therefore, RICLCRE is 0.25% effectiveness (*concluded cases 2018/pending1995-2018*).

5. Government Board of the Federal Administrative Court.

---

[18] Statistical abstract 2018, available in http://transparencia.tribunalesagrarios.gob.mx/index.php/component/k2/item/184
[19] Because of this institutional omission, it was argued RRA 1005/19 case before INAI.

According to Memory 2018[20], in the period from January 1, to December 31, 2018, there are 76,412 stock cases, plus 180,073 received cases and 183,531 concluded legal proceedings, giving a final stock of 62,469 pending cases.

According to President Judge Carlos Chaurand Second Report, the economic amount of legal disputes before the Federal Administrative Court is $619.375 billion, emphasizing no more pending cases[21].

5.1.   Precisions.

- The Federal Administrative Court 2017 RICLCRE was 73.74% (*concluded cases 2017 / received cases 2017 + stock 2017*) and 2018 RICLCRE decreased to 71.56%, which is -2.96% effectiveness.

6. Mexico's Department of Labor and Social Welfare (Labor Law transition).

Because of constitutional labor reform in 2016, according to Secretary Luisa Maria Alcalde Lujan own calculations[22], there are 1´000,000 pending Labor Law cases before Federal Board and State Boards of Conciliation and Arbitration.

6.1.   Precisions.

- Although the Department of Labor and Social Welfare has Open Data, that public information is not functional to disaggregate pending cases and pending cases represented by PROFEDET[23].

7. Judicial Statistics in the 32 states of Mexico: general precisions.

Regarding the Transparency and Access to Public Information, Judicial Statistics in each of the 32 states of the country are produced by:

---

[20]   Memory   2018,   available   in http://www.tfjfa.gob.mx/media/media/memorias/MemoriaAnual2018/index.html

[21]   Press   Report   17/2018,   dated   December   10,   2018,   available   in http://www.tfjfa.gob.mx/sala_prensa/boletin-17-2018/

[22] PRESS NOTE, MVS, January 18 2019, "*A la STPS no le toca quitar o poner líderes sindicales: Luisa María Alcalde*", available in https://mvsnoticias.com/noticias/nacionales/a-la-stps-no-le-toca-quitar-o-poner-lideres-sindicales-luisa-maria-alcalde/

[23] Because of this situation, there were formulated several petitions through INAI.

- 1 Supreme Court of Justice of the State;

- 1 Attorney General;

- 1 Judiciary State Council;

- 1 Board of Conciliation and Arbitration;

- 1 Administrative Court;

- 1 Bureaucratic Labor Court, and

- 1 Alternative Justice Institute.

In some cases, as the State of Guerrero, there are 7 Boards of Conciliation and Arbitration because of the institutional disaggregation of Obligated Authorities[24]. In other instances, likewise the States of Tamaulipas, Yucatan and Oaxaca, there are Municipal Administrative Courts in Victoria City and Merida City; also, an Agrarian Board of Conciliation in Oaxaca City.

Now, it is essential to say that Judicial Statistics, in some cases, have a basis correlated among Obligated Authorities because of functions and institutional faculties. For instance, in Mexico City, while is true that judicial statistics depend directly from the Chief Justice of Supreme Court of Justice of Mexico City in accordance with article 41, clause XI of the Judicial Power of Mexico City Act, the last proposition of the regulation establishes that Judiciary Council will rule the disclosure levels and privileges to Access to Judicial Statistics, according to nature and purposes of information[25].

---

[24] According to the information provided by the Secretary of Labor and Social Welfare of the State of Guerrero, by means of letter DGT / 19/2019 dated February 5, 2019 signed by the General Director of Labor and Social Welfare, the existence of 7 Conciliation and Arbitration Boards in that entity: Local Board of Chilpancingo, Local Board of Zihuatanejo, Local Board of Acapulco 1st, Local Board of Acapulco 2nd, Special Board of Conciliation and Arbitration, Local Board of Iguala and Local Board of Coyuca de Catalan.

[25] Article 41. Corresponds to the Presidency of the Superior Court of Justice of Mexico City: "... XI. Prepare and disseminate the relevant statistical information broken down by categories and categories, either for merely informative purposes, or for the monitoring, control and evaluation of

In another aspect, it is important to reveal that in the State of Morelos, the Judiciary Council became extinct through a Declaration published in the Official Journal "Tierra y Libertad", number 5578 and Decree number 2589 that reforms various provisions of the Political Constitution of the Free and Sovereign State of Morelos, the Organic Administrative Court of Justice Act and the Organic Regulation of Morelos Attorney General, including in the transitory articles TENTH FOURTH and TENTH SEVENTH that legal situation, for which administrative functions are assumed by the Supreme Court of Justice of the State of Morelos.

Regarding to technical disaggregation of Judicial Statistics, it is convenient to say that the information produced by Courts have different customs to generate, to integrate, to conserve and to disseminate data, contrasting the legal prevision of article 70, clause XXX, of the General Transparency and Access to Public Information Act, as well as article 28 Bis of the National System of Statistical and Geographic Information Act, exposing the lack of a basic conceptual framework of judicial statistics, technological tools for data disaggregation, and intelligibility and congruence of the information produced for purposes of Transparency and Public Accountability.

For example, we have the Supreme Court of Justice of the State of Morelos, according to the public information available on its website http://tsjmorelos2.gob.mx/, section INSTITUTION, subparagraph REPORT OF ACTIVITIES, we found the reports of work since 2009; the most recent, 2017-2018, makes mention of various data as a jurisdictional activity, even highlighting that this Court obtained the qualification of 87.4 by the Institute of Public Information and Statistics of Morelos (IMIPE), the first place in all the obligated authorities of the State[26], with 12,176 resolutions in civil and family cases issued in the period 2017-2018. Following, the Supreme Court of Justice the State of Morelos has an official repository of judicial statistics disaggregated at the end of 2018[27], where all of its teenage, family and first instance courts have 89,613 and 4315 pending cases.

---

matters. The Council of the Judiciary will establish the levels of disclosure and privileges of access to it, according to the nature and purposes of the information; "

[26] Available in INFORME DE ACTIVIDADES del Tribunal Superior de Justicia de Morelos, http://tsjmorelos2.gob.mx/2016/wp-content/uploads/2018/05/2do-Informe-TSJMorelos.pdf, page 43.

[27] Available in http://repositoriomorelos.mx/sites/default/files/Poder_Judicial/TSJ/2018/Articulo51/LTAIPEM51_FX XIX_Estadisticas_generadas/2018Diciembre/ANUAL_PARA_TRANSPARENCIA_2018_DIC.pdf

Contrasting these data, the Bureaucratic Labor Court of Jalisco reveals the received complaints[28] in the period 2013-2018.

As we can check from these examples, among the Obligated Authorities, there are technical discrepancies caused by the lack of a basic conceptual framework of Judicial Statistics, avoiding to produce convincing information within the scope of their competences, functions, and faculties. Therefore, it is incomplete, inaccurate, or dark.

Generally, the available information and Judicial Statistics are uploaded on the website of the National Transparency Platform of the obligated authorities, available in the link https://consultapublicamx.inai.org.mx/vut-web/, where the repositories of public information and judicial statistics are free for everyone.

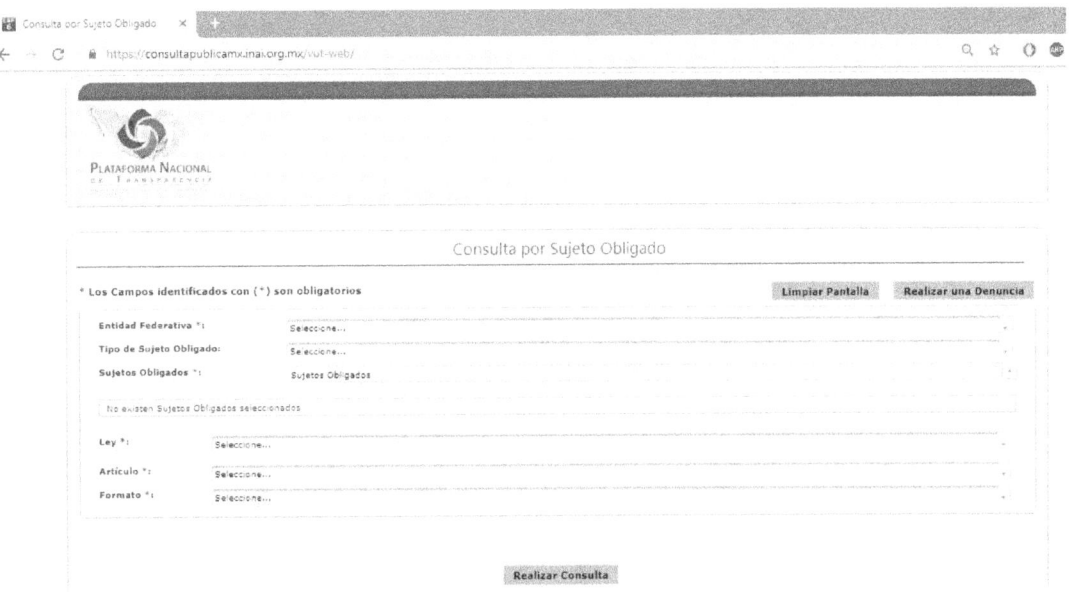

FIGURE 1. PNT PLATFORM. (SCREENSHOT).

---

[28] Available in https://consultapublicamx.inai.org.mx/vut-web/?idSujetoObigadoParametro=3577&idEntidadParametro=17&idSectorParametro=30

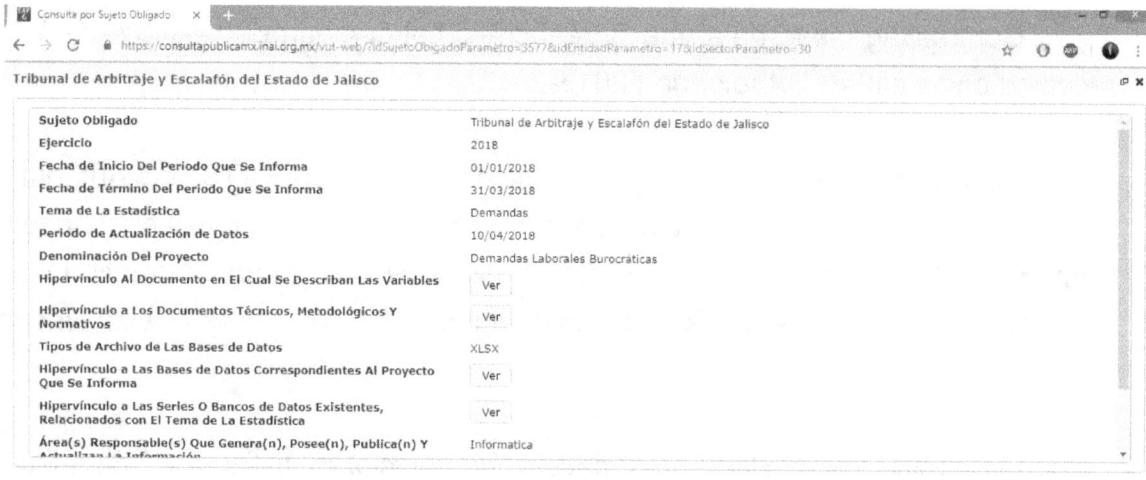

FIGURE 2. AVAILABLE INFORMATION (SCREENSHOT).

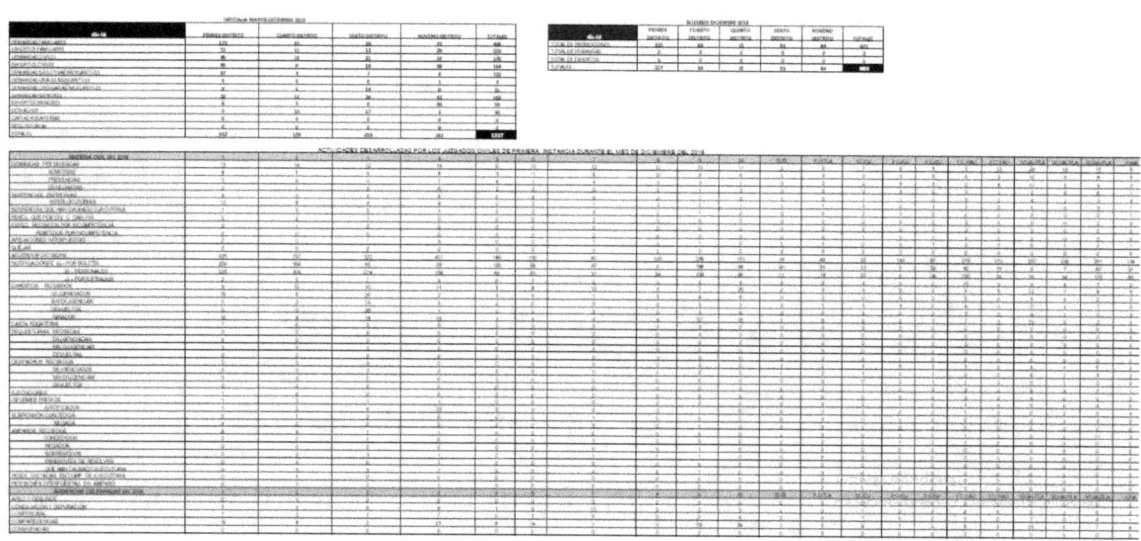

FIGURE 3. JUDICIAL STATISTICS AT SUPREME COURT OF JUSTICE OF STATE OF MORELOS DISAGGREGATION (SCREENSHOT).

8. Judicial Statistics (Summary 2018).

Considering the public information and the available Judicial Statistics, in addition to the explained precisions, we have the following estimates and data:

JURISDICTION	PENDING CASES	% RICLCRE	$$ AMOUNT
FEDERAL JUDICIARY COUNCIL	332,105	75	**
FEDERAL ADMINISTRATIVE COURT	62,469	71.56	$619.365
BUREAUCRATIC LABOR COURT	15,088	0.25	**
HIGHER AGRARIAN COURT	49,900	**	**
DEPARTMENT OF LABOR AND SOCIAL WELFARE (1)	1,000,000	**	**
32 STATE COURTS (2)	3,827,525	24.42***	**
TOTAL	5,287,087	42.81 (3)****	$619.365 (4)
(1) The National estimate of labor law cases in 2019.			
(2) Estimated basis thanks to INEGI National Census 2016 and 2017; including Criminal Law and Alternative Law cases, without Administrative State and Municipal Courts, State Boards and Bureaucratic Labor Courts.			
(3) (Average between available data)			
(4) An estimate of the economic amount in Federal Administrative Courts (BILLION PESOS).			
** Due to the fact that the disaggregated Judicial Statistics of Courts operate, it is not possible to determine the values, just by estimates.			
*** First estimate; real one was 23.36%			
**** RICLCRE real average was 42.54% (-0.27%)			

III. Almanac of Legal Information.

This chapter is a compilation of answers of Obligated Authorities of the Federal Government and the 32 states of Mexico, obtained through the National Transparency Platform. The information was poured, compartmentalized and synthesized.

The chapter is divided by three (*Part A, Part B, and Part C*) following the strategic guidelines explained at this point, and a Summary of petitions and claims.

It is important to emphasize that some Obligated Authorities denied public information and the National Transparency Platform had many technical issues, so the grandfathered INFOMEX software was used to reveal the most pending cases as possible. In some cases, it was required to ask many times the same petition focusing on the core goal and to present claims before the Transparency Regulators, exposing the institutional acquiescence of denying information.

In any case, the full answers and the appendix are available in **Chapter VI. Digital Repository and Bibliography**. Also, petitions and answers are publicly available through the Federal Government, and the 32 states of Mexico grandfathered INFOMEX software.

Part A. Federal Government Legal cases.

1. Constitutional Law cases.

The Supreme Court of Justice of the Nation (SCJN) answered the petition 0330000022719 by Transparency Committee Resolution on February 20, 2019, *INEXISTENCIA DE INFORMACIÓN: CT-I/J-22-2019*; revealing Off. SGA/E/48/2019, dated January 30, 2019:

> *"(...) this General Secretary informs that, within the framework of its statistical powers entrusted to it by the Justices, in terms of Article 67 of the Supreme Court of Justice of the Nation Regulation, does not make a record of records based on the data that is required, so*

it does not have a document under its receipt that contains them, hence the information requested in those terms is non-existent.

Regardless of the above, it should be noted that from the exhaustive search conducted by the Certification and Correspondence Office of this High Court in the legal information system, files related to the request were located, which are made available as guidance, and they are detailed in the table that is attached, in the modality requested. "

The Obligated Authority attaches one Microsoft WORD file with 415 registers where the Federal Government was represented by the Legal Counsel of the President of Mexico and coordinated by Departments and by Legal Units and attorneys of the Federal Government. From the information revealed, there are 113 disaggregated records without resolution:

Federal Government SCJN Legal Cases	
2001-2019	
Type of Legal Case	**Number**
Constitutional Case	5
Amparo Law Direct case	0
Amparo Law Direct appeal	79
Amparo Law Appeal case	3
Jurisdiction case	2
Constitutional Controversy case	3
Thesis Controversy	0
Resolution's Incident of Inquiry	1
Discomfort case.	3
Discomfort appeal case	1
Reclamation appeal case.	0
Petitions to attraction	3
Jurisdiction resumption	2
Various	11
TOTAL	113

Now, the relevance of the answer is not about 415 records and 113 files without resolution, but the absence of regulation to justify SCJN's Statistical System to corroborate the functions, faculties, and competencies by full disaggregation.

SCJN Transparency Committee informs:

"... In this way, as has been maintained in other precedents by this Committee, the existence of the information (and its presumption), as well as the need for its documentation, is conditioned, in any case, by the prior validity of a legal disposition that in general or particular delimits the exercise of the faculties, competences or attributions on the part of the obligated subjects with respect to which the former is requested.

....

...

In this sense, currently in the statistical plane, in which the petition could acquire extension, neither the General Constitution in its article 6, section A, clause V, nor the General Act in its article 70, clause XXX, or the Federal Transparency and Access to Public Information Act in its Article 71, clause V, establish an obligation with these characteristics for the Supreme Court of Justice of the Nation, but only provide that the Federal Judicial Branch must generate statistics in compliance with its faculties, functions or competencies, that allow rendering account of the fulfillment its objectives and its jurisdictional performance, with the most disaggregation degree as possible.

...

Finally, it should be noted that to satisfy the right to access to public information regarding statistical data with a higher degree of disaggregation, for important cases, within the Supreme Court of Justice of the Nation, actions are taken to improve the tools that systematize labor indicators. So that, in the future, it is possible to attend mostly this type of request.

Regardless of the preceding, the General Transparency Unit must send the petitioner the list of files that, in the form of guidance, are made available in the report of the General Secretariat of Agreements, and let him know the electronic link in which he can follow up to the records of interest. "

On the other hand, the Federal Judiciary Council (CJF) answers the petition *0320000053519* by Off. CJF/SECNO/DGEJ/J/648/2019 dated January 31, 2019, informing that, after investigating the SISE Data Base, these are the available records:

AMPARO LAW CASES BEFORE DISTRICT COURTS		
CJEF		
April 2, 2001, to January 23, 2019.		
Decision	**Number**	**%**
Accumulation	1	0.56
Protect	62	34.64
Dismissed	3	1.68
Impediment	3	1.68
Not jurisdiction	16	8.94
Not protect	18	10.06
Not interposed	2	1.18
Not presented	1	0.56
No available	9	5.03
Overrides during trial prosecution	33	18.44
Overrides out of the trial.	23	12.85
Pending	8	4.47
Pending of resolution	0	0
TOTAL (1)	**179**	**100**
Source: CJF		
(1). Information matter of complaint RRA 1530/19 before INAI.		

Considering the answer, it was presented the complaint RRA 1530/19 before the Federal Regulator INAI, grieving that the Obligated Authority indicates 8 files pending and 0 pending of resolution according to SISE Data Base, but in Federal Courts there are many legal cases where the Legal Counsel of the President of Mexico contends; for example, **3,806 Amparo Law cases of Public Officials**

related to Federal Salaries of Public Officials Act, where CJF has the full records of those claims.[29].

It is clear that Mass Media informs the content of those Amparo Law cases, noting Public Officials from Federal Judiciary Branch claiming the President of Mexico[30].

2. Bureaucratic Labor Law cases

The petition 0420000003819 was answered by Off. UT/320/2019 dated March 7, 2019, where the Transparency Unit of Federal Bureaucratic Labor Court (TFCA) informs the cases contended by the Legal Counsel of the President of Mexico and Legal Units of the Federal Government in the period from January 1, 2001 to January 23, 2019. However, the answer is incorrect because TFCA Judicial Statistics at January 2019[31] have these records:

TFCA — EXPEDIENTES ACTIVOS AL 31 DE ENERO DE 2019 POR SALA Y ESTADO PROCESAL

CORTE: 31 DE ENERO DE 2019 — TOTAL DE EXPEDIENTES: **26,308**

SALA	SIN LAUDO		CON LAUDO	CON LAUDO (POR CUMPLIMENTAR)	TOTAL POR SALA
	EN PROCESO (INSTRUCCIÓN)	EN PROYECTO			
PRIEMERA	1,647	559	1,129	594	3,929
SEGUNDA	1,743	667	544	771	3,725
TERCERA	2,207	142	859	679	3,887
CUARTA	1,264	43	1,312	312	2,931
QUINTA	1,490	324	1,162	383	3,359
SEXTA	1,220	201	565	487	2,473
SEPTIMA	1,540	229	849	403	3,021
OCTAVA	1,471	219	201	953	2,844
S.G.A.	113	0	25	1	139
TOTAL	**12,695**	**2,384**	**6,646**	**4,583**	**26,308**
	15,079		**11,229**		

FIGURE 4. TFCA JUDICIAL STATISTICS IN JANUARY 2019.

---

[29] Available in, https://www.animalpolitico.com/2019/01/funcionarios-amparo-ley-remuneraciones/
[30] Available in https://lasillarota.com/jueces-y-magistrados-van-contra-reduccion-de-salarios-acuden-a-scjn/259756
[31] Judicial Statistics available in: http://tfca.gob.mx/work/models/TFCA/Resource/322/1/images/informem_enero2019.pdf

3. Agrarian Law cases.

The petition *3110000002419* was answered by Off. SGA/269/2019 signed by the General Secretary of the Higher Agrarian Court, dated February 11, 2019, informing that in the period from January 1, 2001, to January 23, 2019, there are 771 files where the Federal Government argues by Legal Units and lawyers, with these disaggregated data:

Federal Government Agrarian Law Cases	
January 1, 2001- January 23, 2019	
RESOLUTION	**NUMBER**
Confirms	264
Dismissed	179
Modifies	58
Revokes	218
Not matter	14
Abandoned	2
Unfounded	2
Founded	2
Pending	32
TOTAL	**771**
Source: General Secretary of the Higher Agrarian Court	

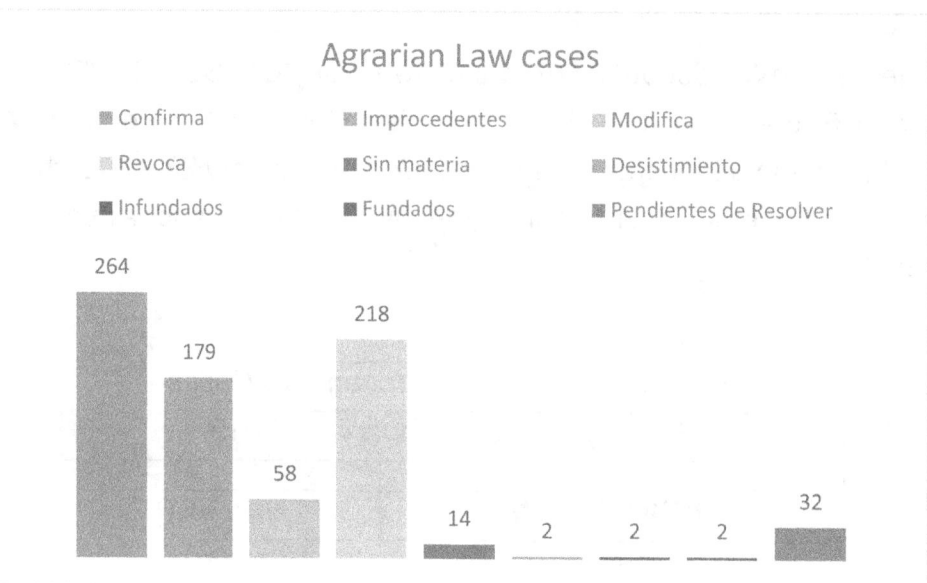

Considering the answer, on February 1, 2019, it was presented the complaint RRA 1013/19 before the Federal Transparency Regulator INAI. The grievance suffered was that the Obligated Authority revealed the existence of 771 contentious cases in the period from January 1, 2001, to January 23, 2019; however, according to its disaggregation of technical information, the sum of the disaggregated cases gives 769 files, not 771. Subsequently, the obliged subject rectified its response, which ultimately concludes the claim.

4. Administrative Law cases.

The Petition *3210000007119* (grandfathered INFOMEX software) was answered by Off. UE-SI-0123/2019 dated February 11, 2019; the Transparency Unit of the Federal Administrative Court informs the Off. JGA-SOTIC-DGSJL-0072/2019 and the Off. JGA-SOTIC-DGSJL-0096/2019 with these disaggregated data:

Federal Government Administrative Law cases			
	Period 2001-2018		
TOTAL CASES			
ATTORNEY	CASES	RESOLUTION	PENDING

LEGAL COUNSEL OF THE PRESIDENT OF MEXICO	84	7	0
FEDERAL GOVERNMENT LEGAL UNITS	67793	57490	5578
TOTAL	67877	57497	5578
	-	-	-
Source: Online Trial General Bureau.			

RESOLUTION DISAGGREGATION								
	Flat and plain nullity	For effects nullity	Partial nullity	OTHER	Dismissed	Partial dismissed and validation	validation	TOTAL
	2	0	0	1	1	1	2	7
	30114	10869	663	424	2002	0	13418	57490
TOTAL	30116	10869	663	425	2003	1	13420	57497
%	52.38	18.9	1.15	0.74	0.34	3.48	23.34	100

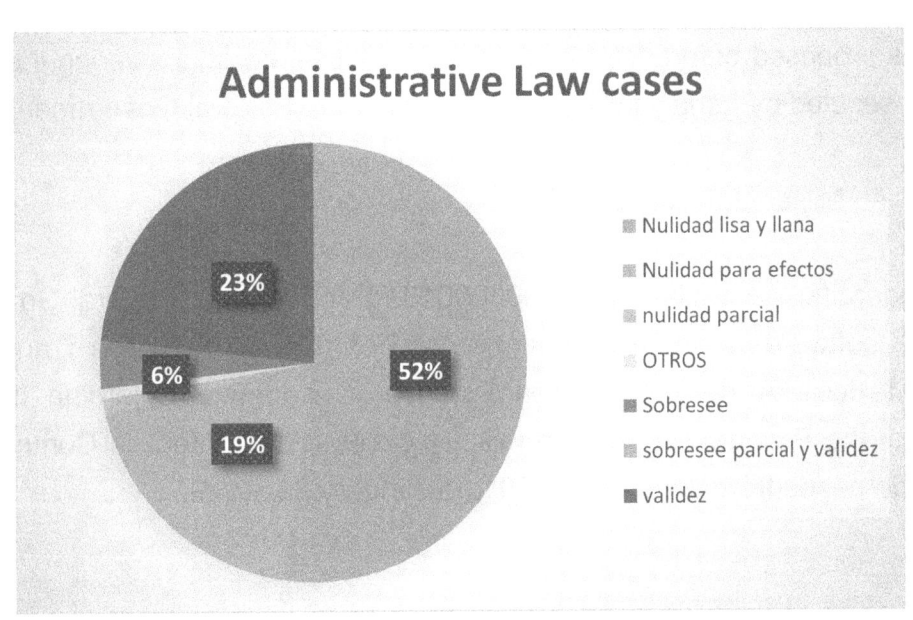

Administrative Law cases

- Nulidad lisa y llana
- Nulidad para efectos
- nulidad parcial
- OTROS
- Sobresee
- sobresee parcial y validez
- validez

5. Civil Law cases.

Regarding the petition *0320000053519*, by Off. CJF/SECNO/DGEJ/J/648/2019 dated January 31, 2019, the General Bureau of Judicial Statistics of the Federal Judiciary Council informs that in SISE DataBase there is one Civil Law/ Administrative Law case where the Legal Counsel of the President of Mexico argues in the period April 2, 2001-January 23, 2019. Therefore, the complaint RRA 1530/19 was promoted before INAI grieving the absence of a complete answer.

6. Criminal Law cases.

Regarding the petition 0001700036419 (grandfathered Federal Government INFOMEX software), by Off. FGR/UTAG/DG/001296/2019 dated February 20, 2019, the Transparency Unit of the Attorney General of the Republic informs *"... the administrative units indicated with attention were coincident in stating that after carrying out an exhaustive and reasonable search in their archives, they found no records inherent to complaints and complaints made by the Legal Department of the Federal Executive, on behalf of the Head of the Federal Executive Branch, during the period from January 1, 2001 to January 23, 2019, therefore, does not have available data of the same ... ".*

Considering the answer of the Obligated Authority, the complaint RRA 1884/19 is proposed before INAI because of the absence of answering the criminal cases prosecuted by Legal Units and attorneys of the Federal Government.

7. Military Law cases.

Regarding the petition 0000700030019 (grandfathered Federal Government INFOMEX software), by Answer Sheet dated February 6, 2019; the Transparency Unit of Mexico's Army informs *nonexistence* of evidence regarding the Legal Counsel of the President of Mexico military cases represented as Commander in Chief in the period from January 1, 2001, to January 23, 2019.

8. International Law cases.

Regarding the petition 0000500020719, by Off. UDT-1226/2019 dated February 19, 2019, the Transparency Unit of Mexico's Department of Foreign Affairs communicates that all information is available in https://datos.gob.mx. Also, the Obligated Authority informs about the cases *Avena and other Nationals (Mexico v. United States of America)* and *Request for Interpretation of the Judgement of March 31, 2004, in the Case concerning Avena and Other Mexican Nationals (Mexico v. United States of America)*, before the International Court of Justice; also 12 human rights cases before the Inter American Court of Human Rights, noting *"...the cost of legal representation of the two cases before the International Court of Justice, it is reported pro bono; and in the cases before the Inter-American Court of Human Rights, the legal representation of the Mexican State was made directly by the Ministry of Foreign Affairs (SRE). "*

Furthermore, the Obligated Authority says that there is *United Mexican States v. BP Exploration & Production Inc, et al. Case 2:13-cv-01441*, at US Louisiana East District Court, where an extrajudicial agreement was celebrated with BP by a sum of USD 25.5 million, in exchange to Mexico Government abandonment of the case against the Oil corporation. Shulte, Roth & Zable LLP represented Mexico and received payments from the Federal Budget.

According to Mexico's Department of Foreign Affairs Open Data, the disaggregated information in Civil Law, Criminal Law, and Administrative Law, dated December 31, 2019, Mexico had 170,261 Consular Protection petitions worldwide and 185,031 Consular Assistance petitions in the period 2013-2018. Similarly, Mexico had 58 lawyers in the United States of America and 35 worldwide for Consular Assistance topics. Furthermore, 1095 Mexicans were arrested during 2018 around the World.

Nevertheless, Open Data does not precise pending cases in the United States of America and the complete disaggregation of Civil Law, Administrative Law, and Criminal Law cases. It is true that the Obligated Authority reports attended cases as Open Data, but does not pronounce about pending cases charged to Federal Budget to defend Mexicans worldwide.

Besides, it is convenient to say that the Obligated Authority does report the legal cases before the Inter American Court of Human Rights, but does not inform about Lydia Cacho's legal case before UNHRC, where Mexico recognized its responsibility with a public excuse.

According to the Inter American Commission of Human Rights Statistics, closing 2017, there were 1584 open cases at least against Mexico, in addition to 11,565 pending petitions to proceed[32]. On the other side, two pending cases before UNHRC[33] had the United Nations Statistics.

Finally, it is essential to say that Mexico's Department of State does not reveal information regarding Arbitration from January 1st, 2000 to January 23, 2019, and pending cases, besides the existence of *Thunderbird* case[34] and 2013 *PEMEX*'s case[35]. Regarding US lawyers that represent Mexico, there is the case that Thomas Goldstein, from Goldstein & Russell P.C., has as a client to Mexico[36].

Therefore, the claim RRA 1903/19 was promoted before INAI.

Immediately, by Official Letter No. UDT-4296/2019 dated May 29, 2019, the Transparency Unit of the Ministry of Foreign Affairs reports the following:

> *"In response to the instruction of the Plenary of the INAI, the following is informed:*
>
> *1. The General Directorate for the Protection of Mexicans Abroad (DGPME), dated May 27, 2019, through email number. PME105806.19, stated the following:*
>
> *"In this regard, communications PME101651.19, PME103151.19 and PME103477.19, dated January 24, 2019, March 14, 2019 and March 22, 2019, respectively, through which*

---

[32] Available in http://www.oas.org/es/cidh/multimedia/estadisticas/estadisticas.html,

[33] Available in https://www.ohchr.org/en/hrbodies/ccpr/pages/ccprindex.aspx

[34] Available in http://www.2006-2012.economia.gob.mx/eventos-noticias/sala-de-prensa/comunicados/5439-mxico-gana-arbitraje-internacional,

[35] Available in https://www.proceso.com.mx/379209/la-derrota-de-pemex-ante-siemens-le-cuesta-500-millones-de-dolares

[36] Available in http://www.goldsteinrussell.com/representative-clients/

this General Directorate is attached provided to that Transparency Unit all the information required by the interested party.

It is important to note that it is noted that the complementary information that this General Directorate provided through the aforementioned communication PME103477.19 dated March 22, 2019, was not considered in the aforementioned resolution of the INAI.

This information contains the number of cases of Mexican people to whom Mexico's diplomatic and consular network abroad provided assistance and / or consular protection from January 1, 2001 to December 31, 2009. This information is broken down. by year, country (jurisdiction or foreign country where the legal problem was presented), scope (nature of the legal problem) and status of the case (pending or concluded, that is, the meaning of the resolution of such matters).

It should be stressed that the consular and diplomatic network of Mexico records the cases considering the aspects that people face when they request assistance and consular protection, according to the areas in which it is classified: administrative, civil, human rights, immigration, labor and criminal . However, the support provided by the consulates and the follow-up of the cases depends on the consular assistance requested by Mexican persons and the powers conferred by the regulations in force in this matter.

This consular assistance may or may not be related to the legal process, since the Mexican person deprived of his or her freedom can request any type of assistance as financial support for essential items, medical or psychological care, among other requests.

For example, detainees may request consular assistance because they consider that the medical care they receive in prison is poor and authorize the consulate to carry out procedures on their behalf and, at the same time, do not require legal assistance or guidance.

Although one of the obligations of the consular network is to ensure that the rights of Mexican people are respected, including "due process," it is essential to underline that consular assistance and protection is provided at the request of the party and is the national itself. The one that determines the type of support you require, and is not always the follow-up to your legal cases.

Due to the above, the cases of consular assistance are concluded at the moment in which the request of the national was favorably addressed. Hence, the meaning of the resolution is reflected in the status of the case (pending or concluded). "

Additionally, the DGPME attached five (05) files, which contains information regarding legal matters raised by Mexicans abroad from 2001 to January 23, 2019, which has the following breakdown: a) Nature of the legal problem, b) Jurisdiction or foreign country where the legal problem was presented, c) The meaning of the resolution of said matters, d) Matters pending resolution.

2. The General Directorate for Human Rights and Democracy (DGDHD), dated May 28, 2019, through email No. DDH02103, stated the following:

"This General Directorate sends a couple of informative tables on all the matters that the Mexican State maintains before various international organizations of a quasi-jurisdictional nature, namely: the UN Human Rights Committee, Committee for the Elimination of Discrimination against UN woman, UN Committee against Torture, the Committee on the Rights of Persons with Disabilities of the UN and the Inter-American Commission on Human Rights of the OAS. The tables include the breakdown requested by the INAI in its resolution.

Regarding the pending cases before the Inter-American Commission, it is pertinent to clarify that, as the applicant states on page 33 of the INAI resolution (attached), 1584 matters related to Mexico are pending before the Inter-American Human Rights System. The confusion may be due to the fact that the Commission has indicated that, at the end of 2018, it had 1,996 petitions pending initial study. It should be noted that when the Commission receives the petitions, it carries out an initial pre-admissibility study, which means that not all of these matters are processed; Only those cases that meet the minimum requirements established in its Regulations, are transferred and notified to the State concerned.

The above can be corroborated on the website of the Inter-American Commission, in the following link: http://www.oas.org/es/cidh/multimedia/estadisticas/estadisticas.html ". (Sic)

Additionally, the DGDHD attached two (02) files in Excel format, which contains information on the legal matters in which Mexico is a part, including quasi-jurisdictional international organizations such as the UN Human Rights Committee and the Inter-American Commission on Human Rights of the OAS, which has the following breakdown: a) Nature of the legal problem, b) The counterpart of each legal case, c) The meaning of the resolution, d) The issues that are pending resolution, e) Legal signature I of lawyers who represented Mexico in these processes and amount of perceptions issued for said services.

In that sense, annexes sent by the DGPME and the DGDHD are attached to this, giving strict compliance with the instruction of the Plenary of the INAI. "

Finally, it is pertinent to say that Mexico holds at least 10 international arbitrations in dispute before the International Center for Settlement of

Investment Disputes (CIADI-ICSID) of the World Bank, for an amount exceeding $ 6,000 million[37]. The cases are:

Case No.	Claimant(s)	Respondent(s)	Status
ARB/19/26	Terence Highlands	United Mexican States	Pending
UNCT/18/4	Alicia Grace and others	United Mexican States	Pending
ARB/19/1	Legacy Vulcan, LLC	United Mexican States	Pending
UNCT/18/5	PACC Offshore Services Holdings Ltd	United Mexican States	Pending
ARB(AF)/17/3	Vento Motorcycles, Inc.	United Mexican States	Pending
ARB(AF)/17/2	Eutelsat S.A.	United Mexican States	Pending
UNCT/17/1	Joshua Dean Nelson	United Mexican States	Pending
ARB(AF)/16/3	B-Mex, LLC and others	United Mexican States	Pending
ARB(AF)/15/2	Lion Mexico Consolidated L.P.	United Mexican States	Pending

9. Human Rights cases.

Regarding the petition 0000400030319, by Off. UDDH/911/ETyAI/054/2019 dated February 7, 2019, Mexico's Department of State Human Rights Unit informs that it has not faculties regarding legal representation before the Inter American Commission of Human Rights, where Mexico's Department of State is responsible.

Independently, the Obligated Authority responds that Mexico's Department of State follows the Inter American Court of Human Rights decisions accomplishment,

---

[37] Available in CIADI https://icsid.worldbank.org/sp/Pages/cases/AdvancedSearch.aspx; also "AMLO heredó litigios que superan los 6 mil mdd", REPORTE ÍNDIGO, October 3, 2019, available in http://www.ejecentral.com.mx/lopez-obrador-heredo-litigios-que-superan-los-6-mil-mdd/

where the legal cases that Mexico has been responsible for human rights violations. Moreover, the Authority reports about the First Report of International Recommendations of Human Rights (2000-2018)[38].

Then, it is promoted the claim RRA 1463/19 before INAI because article 24 of Mexico's Department of Government Regulation establishes that *"...The Unit for the Defense of Human Rights shall have the following attributions: I. Coordinate, guide and monitor the work and tasks of protection and defense of human rights carried out by the dependencies and entities of the Federal Public Administration.".*

Moreover, the claim grieves by incorrect information because of Lydia Cacho's public recognition in January 2019.

Later, the Obligated Authority rectifies answer by Off. UGAJ/UT/093/2019 dated February 28, 2019, revealing: *"... (11) sentences, forty-six (46) petitions, twenty-one (21) cases and eight (8) in-depth reports in the inter-American human rights system and one (1) matter before the United Nations Human Rights Committee".*

On the other hand, regarding the petition 3510000007919 (grandfathered INFOMEX Federal Government software), by Off.09404 dated February 21, 2019, the General Bureau of Claims and Transparency of the National Commission of Human Rights informs these disaggregated data:

National Commission of Human Rights (claims)			
January 1, 2001, to January 23, 2019.			
Authority	**Claims**	**Concluded**	**Pending**
President of Mexico	102	100	2
Federal Public Officials	126,250	121622	4628
Source. General Bureau of Claims and Transparency.			

---

[38] Available in http://recomendacionesdh.mx/

Federal Public Officials	
Claims disaggregation	
Resolution	**Number**
Orientation	53833
During procedure	39584
Not matter	14924
Accumulation	3849
Conciliation	3433
Lack of Personal interest	2839
Withdrawal	1466
Recommendation	913
Not Jurisdiction	569
Adjustment to State HRC.	194
Severe HR Recommendation	17
General Recommendation	1
TOTAL	121622

President of Mexico	
Claims disaggregation	
Resolution	**Number**
Orientation	38
During the procedure	32
Not matter	13
Lack of personal interest	7
Accumulation	3
Conciliation	3
Not jurisdiction	2
Adjustment to State HRC	1
Sever HR recommendation	1
TOTAL	100

On other hand, regarding the petition 0000500020719 (grandfathered INFOMEX Federal Government software), by Off. UDT-1226/2019 dated February 19, 2019, the Transparency Unit of Mexico's Department of Foreign Affairs informs *Avena and other Nationals (Mexico v. United States of America* and *Request for Interpretation of the Judgement of March 31, 2004, in the case concerning Avena and Other Mexican Nationals (Mexico v. United States of America*), before the International Court of Justice; also, 12 human rights cases before the Inter American Court of Human Rights, where *"...... in what it represents at of the legal representation of the two cases before the International Court of Justice, it is reported that it was made pro bono; and in the case of the cases before the Inter-American Court of Human Rights, the legal representation of the Mexican State was made directly by the Ministry of State (SRE)"*. That answer was disputed by claim RRA 1903/19 before INAI.

Finally, it is convenient to specify the content of the email received on April 5, 2019 from the Office of the United Nations High Commissioner for Human Rights:

"Dear Mr. Remes,

The data depends on which committee you refer to.

The Human Rights Committee has registered 8 cases, of which 2 have already been decided.

The CEDAW Committee has registered a case.
The CRPD Committee has registered a case.
The Committee against Torture has registered 3 cases, and has decided on one case.

If you refer to the Committee of Enforced Disappearances and its mechanism of urgent actions, in that framework there have been 468 urgent actions of which 23 have been closed.

You can find the opinions of the committees at: https://juris.ohchr.org/

Sincerely,

Petitions and Inquiries Section (Section des requêtes et des enquêtes) Office of the United Nations High Commissioner for Human Rights Palais des Nations ".

10. Mexico's important legal cases.

Regarding the petition 0220000005319, by Off. 12C.126/219 dated March 11, 2019; the Transparency Unit of the Legal Counsel of the President of Mexico informs:

"... the Deputy Council of Consultation and Constitutional Studies and the Deputy Ministry of Legislation and Regulatory Studies, through the Official Letters 3.0469/2019 and 4.0482/2019, submitted the information reported by various agencies of the Federal Public Administration in response to what was indicated in the Circular Letter issued by the Legal Counsel of the the President of Mexico, published in the Official Journal of the Federation on December 10, 2019.

With regard to the statements made by the Deputy Council for Constitutional Control and Litigation, through the Off. 5.0702/2019, reported that regarding the contentious issues that were sent by the Units responsible for legal support of the various agencies and entities of the Federal Public Administration to the Legal Counsel of the President of Mexico, according to the Circular Letter published in the Official Journal of the Federation on December 10, 2019, indicated that the number amounts to 16,979 cases.

Likewise, he pointed out that the information regarding the "Dependency / Entities of the Federal Public Administration, data of identification of trials, counterpart, matter, reason of relevance, procedural status, prospective, suggestions and observations", the same work in a system that contains data that are part of a deliberative process of public servants whose access is restricted, in that it includes recommendations, points of view, opinions and suggestions on contentious issues that is currently in operation, that is, the information contained in said system is located in the case of exceptions provided by clause VIII, article 113, General Transparency and Access to Information Act for which reason it requests to classify the information for a period of 5 years, in terms of the articles 113, clauses VIII and XI of the General Transparency and Access to Public Information Act; article 98, clause I, 100 and 110, clauses VIII and XI of the Federal Transparency and Access to Public Information Act.

In response to the statements made by the Deputy Council for Constitutional Control and Litigation, the Transparency Committee of the Legal Counsel of the President of Mexico, in the Fifth Extraordinary Session, dated March 6, 2019, indicated that it is competent to know and decide on the request, so in terms of the provisions of articles 44, Clause II and 137, paragraph a) of the General Transparency and Access to Public Information Act, 65, Clause II and 140, clause I of the Federal Transparency and Access to Public Information Act, confirms the classification of the information as reserved requested by the Deputy Council for Constitutional Control and Contentious, for the foregoing, it is useful to find attached to this copy of the above-mentioned offices, as well as the resolution issued by the Transparency Committee. "

Well, according to the revealed information, the Legal Counsel of the President of Mexico has 67 reported cases, 51 Regulation projects, and 16 Law drafts. On the other hand, the Obligated Authority informs of 62 cases that will be presented to the President of Mexico for deliberation.

Spotlights the 16,979 relevant legal cases which are classified regarding the disaggregated data for five years. Because of this proposition, it is purposed a claim before INAI, case RRA 2704/19, where the classified information was revoked and put in the same in the modality of direct consultation, through a computer located on the third floor of the National Palace.

Part B. Federal Government and the 32 states of Mexico pending cases.

1. Federal Courts.

   i. Federal Judiciary Council (CJF).

Regarding the petition 0320000063019 (grandfathered INFOMEX Federal Government software), by Off. CJF/SECNO/DGEJ/J/844/2019 dated February 6, 2019, the manager of the General Bureau of Judicial Statistics informs these data in an EXCEL file:

Court	Case law	Pending cases (Until February 8, 2019)		TOTAL
		April 2, 2001- December 31, 2009, period.	January 1, 2010- February 8, 2019, period.	
CRIMINAL JUSTICE CENTERS	Criminal case	-	38,823	38,823
DISTRICT COURTS	Amparo case	49,012	89,986	138,998
	Criminal case	25,893	38,686	64,579
	Civil and administrative cases	1,113	15,780	16,893
UNITARY COURTS	Amparo Case	96	1,033	1,129
	Criminal appeal case	826	2,491	3,317
	Civil and administrative appeal case	111	1,134	1,245

COLLEGIATE CIRCUIT COURTS	**Amparo case**	2,509	113,142	**115,651**
	Amparo appeal case	2,795	65,879	**68,674**
	Amparo complaint case	832	14,184	**15,016**
TOTAL		83,187	381,138	464,325

According to *April 2, 2001- December 31, 2009* period data, there are 4 pending cases that started before December 31, 1999: case 5/1998 of the Fifth Administrative "A" District Court at Mexico City, case 171/1999 of the Seventh Administrative "A" District Court at Mexico City, case 1/1996 of the Second District Court at Quintana Roo and case 2/98 of the Third Administrative "B" District Court in Mexico City. On the other hand, there are 355 administrative law pending cases of the Federal Government.

Moreover, in the period *January 1, 2010- February 8, 2019*, there are 14 administrative cases with litigation economic amount of $319,223,076.42.

Finally, in 12,618 administrative, civil and labor law pending cases, there is a litigation economic amount of $97, 696, 465,511.73.

In another aspect, regarding the petition 0320000102319, by Off. 354/2019 dated March 1, 2019, the Third Member and President of the Single Substantiation Commission informs these cases:

Federal Judiciary Council		
Year	Received	Concluded
2014	88	88
2015	103	103
2016	96	96
2017	104	97
2018	97	37
2019	23	0

In Process February 19, 2019.	55	Pending.	90

ii.   Federal Bureaucratic Labor Court.

According to Judicial Statistics disaggregated to January 2019[39], the Federal Bureaucratic Labor Court has these pending cases:

PENDING CASES			
Before Dec. 31, 1999	Jan. 1, 2000, to Dec. 31, 2010	Jan. 1, 2011- Act	**TOTAL**
3	1823	13,253	15,079

Similarly, the Bureaucratic Federal Court informs about these pending accomplishment cases:

COMPLIANCE PENDING CASES
4583

iii.   Mexico's Army- Military Courts.

Regarding the petition 0000700056519 (grandfathered INFOMEX Federal Government software) by Answer Sheet dated February 27th, 2019, signed by the Transparency Unit of Mexico's Army Chief, revealing "*we inform you that we do not have the information with the level of detail required ... However, based on the principle of maximum publicity, you are provided with the following electronic address where you will be able to consult the information you require ...*", attaching the algorithm to proceed with the information through INAI software[40].

---

[39]   Available   in
http://tfca.gob.mx/work/models/TFCA/Resource/322/1/images/informem_enero2019.pdf
[40]   Available   in   https://consultapublicamx.inai.org.mx/vut-
web/?idSujetoObigadoParametro=3577&idEntidadParametro=17&idSectorParametro=30

iv. Federal Board of Conciliation and Arbitration.

Regarding the petition *1410000006319* (grandfathered INFOMEX Federal Government software), by Off. 110/SSI/1410000006319/2019 dated February 26, 2019, the Transparency Unit reveals these pending cases:

Federal Board of Conciliation and Arbitration			
Before Dec. 31, 1999	Jan. 1, 2000, to Dec. 31, 2010	Jan. 1, 2011,- Act	**TOTAL**
2,757	71,279	36,0882	434,981

v. Mexico's Department of Labor and Social Welfare/ Office of the Defense of Labor.

Regarding the petition *1411100006419* (grandfathered INFOMEX Federal Government software) PROFEDET (*Office of the Defense of Labor*) declares not jurisdiction, informing that the Federal Board of Conciliation and Arbitration is the correct Obligated Authority to answer.

Considering that the article 530 of the Federal Labor Act establishes that PROFEDET has the faculty to *"Represent or advise workers and their unions, whenever they request it, before any authority, in matters related to the application of labor standards; II. File the ordinary and extraordinary resources coming, for the defense of the worker or union; and III. To propose to the interested parties friendly solutions for the settlement of their conflicts and to record the results in authorized minutes";* despite the fact that the Obligated Authority has institutional records since 1929, the claim RRA 1461/19 is argued before INAI.

Well, the Plenary of the INAI revoked the response granted by the obligated subject, including, of course, an Excel file containing the matters sponsored by PROFEDET under the Federal Expenditure Budget:

PROFEDET			
Before December 31, 1999	From Jan 1 2000 to December 31, 2010	Jan 1, 2011- ACT	**TOTAL**
67	7,923	49,240	57,230

Pending cases charged to Federal Budget (Budget paradox)	
21,492	37.55%

It is is important to note that the oldest issue sponsored by PROFEDET dates from May 31, 1995, is in Mexico City at the Federal Board 9 Bis and consists of a Pension and work risks dispute.

On the other hand, regarding the petition 0001400018119, by Off. STPS/UT/181/19 dated February 27, 2019, the Manager of Evaluation, Public Accountability and Responsibility of Mexico's Department of Labor and Social Welfare informs the Off. 312/1.4/01/001/2019 dated February 8, 2019, revealing that"... *according to the powers granted to each Administrative Unit by the Internal Regulations of the Ministry of Labor and Social Security (STPS) and specifically Article 21, this General Directorate has no powers to carry out the registration of claimed benefits and proceedings. In this sense, this Administrative Unit agrees with the response granted by the General Directorate of Legal Affairs (DGAJ).* "

Considering that the Obligated Authority has the information required, it is argued before INAI the claim RRA 2178/19, where the answer is modified.

vi.   Higher Agrarian Court.

Regarding the petition 3110000003119, by Off. SGA/235/2019 dated January 30, 2019, the General Secretary of the Higher Agrarian Court informs that the information is available at *http://doctransp.tribunalesagrarios.gob.mx/share/s/Da8X5HgnS3OPq2oDVHIQOw.*

In respect of *ADRLC, the General Secretary says that terms are established* in Agrarian Act, Chapter III, Agrarian trial procedure, articles 178 to 190.

According to its Judicial Statistics[41], it warns a synthesis of the jurisdictional activity from July 21, 1992, to June 30, 2018, as seen as follows:

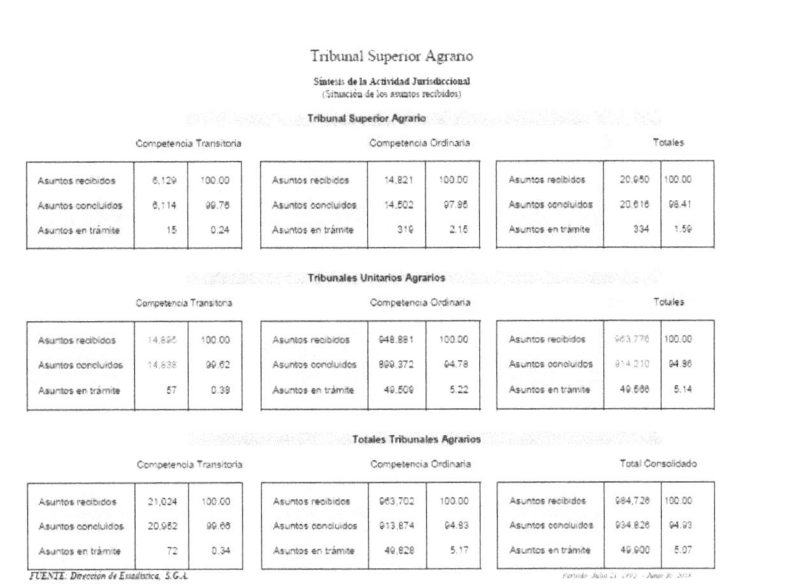

FIGURE 5. Higher Agrarian Court Statistics.

According to the available information, the Judicial Statistics from the Higher Agrarian Court does not have a complex disaggregation degree according to General and Federal Transparency Acts, so that Public Accountability in reason to functions, faculties, and competencies might be fulfilled. In contrast, its Judicial Statistics have a disaggregation degree focused on Amparo cases, "*traveling justice*" and a catalog of petitions answered, but not a necessary disaggregation order by year, to know in the period 1992-2018 either the agrarian cases and the Court, as well as the litigation economic amount, especially when 49,900 pending cases are revealed.

Because of the content of the answer, the claim RRA 1005/19 was promoted before INAI, so that the Obligated Authority may reveal the complete disaggregation from its Judicial Statistics and the pending cases in the 3 periods of time (cases before December 31, 1999; from January 1, 2000, to December 31, 2010, and January 1, 2011, to current day).

---

[41] Available in *http://doctransp.tribunalesagrarios.gob.mx/share/s/Da8X5HgnS3OPq2oDVHlQOw*

vii. Federal Administrative Court.

Regarding the petition 3210000009219, by Off. UE-SI-0154/2019 dated February 14, 2019, the Transparency Unit Chief of the Federal Administrative Court informs about the following disaggregated information:

Federal Administrative Court pending cases		
Year	Cases	Economic amount
2004	1	$82,709.48
2006	2	-
2007	3	$8,066,227.11
2008	1	-
2009	11	$112,192,387.61
2010	8	$21,696.30
2011	32	$43,517,083.69
2012	46	$524,698,649.76
2013	70	$3,388,198,555.18
2014	162	$2,176,150,239.64
2015	471	$11,830,452,958.90
2016	1912	$27,114,529,094.06
2017	7133	$78,653,561,834.89
2018	54314	$248,264,450,779.76
In white	197	-
TOTAL.	64363	$372,115,922,216.38

Source. General Bureau of online Trial.

ADRLC

Procedure	Days
Ordinary	268
Summary	93

Source. General Bureau of online Trial.

viii. Attorney General of the Republic.

Regarding the petition 0001700076619, by Off. FGR/UTAG/DG/002033/2019 dated March 20, 2019, the Director of the Transparency Unit informs the following pending criminal cases data:

TCJS				NCJS			
CURRENT	PENDING	RESERVE	TOTAL	TEMPORARY FILE	DELAYED	RESERVE	TOTAL
21,851	14,129	133	36,133	61,098	40,863	7,375	109,336

However, it is convenient to say that, in a press conference, the Attorney General of the Republic informed of the existence of a lag of more than 300 thousand pending criminal cases[42].

2. Aguascalientes.

i. Governor of Aguascalientes.

Regarding the petition 00060919, by Resolution dated February 19, 2019, Transparency Unit Chief informs that General Department of Government of Aguascalientes is the Obligated Authority to answer the motion.

ii. General Department of Government.

Regarding the petition 00036519, by Resolution dated February 20, 2019, the Transparency Unit Chief of the General Department of Government of Aguascalientes informs the existence of pending cases before the Board of Conciliation and Arbitration and the Bureaucratic Labor Court:

	LABOR LAW CASES			BUREAUCRATIC LABOR LAW			
Jurisdiction	Before Dec.	Jan. 1, 2000,	Jan. 1,	Before Dec. 31, 1999	Jan. 1, 2000, to	Jan. 1, 2011,- Act	TOTAL

---

[42] LE HEREDAN REZAGO A LA FISCALÍA, El Heraldo de México, 7 de mayo del 2019, available in https://heraldodemexico.com.mx/pais/le-heredan-rezago-en-la-fiscalia/

	31, 1999	to Dec. 31, 2010	2011,- Act		Dec. 31, 2010		
Aguascalientes	0	656	7288	0	15	1992	9951

In respect of ADRLC, the Obligated Authority informs that ... *the resolution of the cases before our jurisdiction, is entirely variable, since on average we ventilate a total of 20 procedures, of which the internal areas manage their time to meet them, hence as such an average time it is not possible to establish, for example, a labor trial for unjustified dismissal can last up to 3 years, or, a couple of months, because the parties agreed to its conclusion. "*

Moreover, the authority explains that "... *It is difficult to determine the duration of the labor trials that correspond to the H. Arbitration Court, since it depends on the procedural impulse that the plaintiff promotes within its file; we have lawsuits that are adjusted to legal times, that is, in 9 months they are resolved, and as reported in this report request we have records that were generated in 2010 and have not yet concluded, or are in the execution process".*

iii. Department of Administration.

Regarding the petition 00061019, by Resolution dated February 20, 2019, the Transparency Unit of the Department of Administration declares its manifest non-jurisdiction, specifying that the correct Authority is the General Department of Government.

iv. Supreme Court of Justice of the State of Aguascalientes.

Regarding the petition 00036419, by resolution *PROCEDIMIENTO DE ACCESO A LA INFORMACIÓN PAI. PJE. 0039/2019* dated February 18, 2019, the Transparency Unit of the Supreme Court of Justice of the State of Aguascalientes informs a Data Base with the following disaggregation:

Pending cases
Supreme Court of Justice of the State of Aguascalientes

Disaggregation	Number
Before December 31, 1999	2,652
From January 1, 2000 to December 31 2010	16,720
From January 1, 2011-actually	85,054
Oral	898
Criminal Traditional System	1,818
Mix	16,033
Orality	2,157
TOTAL	125,332

Source. Informatics Bureau of the Supreme Court of Justice of the State of Aguascalientes.

Considering the information revealed by the Obligated Authority, it is essential to say that in the First Commercial Court there is one inheritance dispute, case 0474/1945 with more than 70 years pending of resolution. Moreover, there are 89 cases with more than 50 years pending of resolution; 6 from the 1950s and 83 from the 1960s.

v. Aguascalientes Attorney General.

Regarding the petition 00072219, by resolution PNT.089.072219/2019 dated February 26, 2019, the Transparency Unit of Aguascalientes Attorney General informs the data of pending criminal cases under prosecution:

Jurisdiction		TCJS			NCJS		
		Temporary file	Pending	SUBTOTAL	Temporary file	Pending	SUBTOTAL
Aguascalientes		8626	19399	28025	19692	23417	43109

As a matter of interest, the Obligated Authority says that the National Census of State Justice Procuration 2019 has validated the information related to criminal cases. Moreover, there are pending to prove 2018 Criminal Cases; therefore, when INEGI finishes this data, it will be published.

3. Baja California.

    i. Supreme Court of Justice of the State of Baja California.

Regarding the petition 00084519, by Off. 437/UT/MXL/2019 dated March 6, 2019, the Transparency Unit of the Supreme Court of Justice of the State of Baja California informs several papers related to Criminal, Civil, Family and Mixed Judges, in the District of Mexicali, Tijuana, Ensenada, and San Quintin, attaching the proper information.

From the legal cases informed, in the Third Civil Court of Tijuana there are the cases 788/1972 (Civil executive), 2784/1975 and 1648/1977 (Civil ordinary). Moreover, in the Second Civil Court of Baja California, there is the case 00970/1970 (intestate inheritance).

Now, according to the revealed information by judicial statistics, the Obligated Authority details 193,149 pending cases, 181,596 civil, familiar and teenage law cases, and 11,553 criminal law cases. However, the judicial statistics and the disaggregated attached files have these data findings[43]:

Supreme Court of Justice of the State of Baja California pending cases			
Year	Received	Concluded	Pending cases
2018	73,224	46,225	26,999
2017	61,254	54,427	6,827
2016	66,292	67,831	-1,539
2015	71,385	71,753	-368
2014	66,636	50,868	15,768
2013	66,265	52,018	14,247
2012	64,451	49,369	15,082
2011	63,367	50,256	13,111
2010	67,237	54,182	13,055
2009	68,965	47,774	21,191
2008	69,181	53,365	15,816
2007	65,168	48,416	16,752

---

[43] Available in http://transparencia.pjbc.gob.mx/paginas/estadisticas.aspx

2006	49,446	25,850	23,590
2005	61822	31,862	29,960
2004	-	57,197	-
2003	59838	28,564	31,274
Compartmentalized cases**			**+35078**
TOTAL			**276,843**
** Data obtained by comparing judicial statistics 2006 and 2007, available in http://transparencia.pjbc.gob.mx/paginas/estadisticas.aspx			

Furthermore, we can precise that the **RICLCRE** from the Obligated Authority is **17.16% effectiveness** (*concluded cases 2018/ received cases 2018 + pending cases 1970 to 2017*).

ii. Administrative State Court of Baja California.

On February 18, 2019, an appeal is argued before the Institute of Transparency and Access to Public Information for the State of Baja California regarding the petition 00084619 because the obligated subject places the status FINISHED on the National Transparency Platform said request without attaching any response or proof of the steps taken.

Similarly, on March 5, 2019, a second appeal is insisted on petition 00140119 in which the obligated person reiterates said refusal.

Then, in the resolution of the Appeal REV / 062/2019 dated September 10, 2019, the Institute of Transparency and Access to Public Information of Baja California revoked the response to request 00084619, instructing the subject to disclose forced information consistent with the lawsuits pending resolution.

By Off. dated September 26, 2019, the First Clerk of the Acting Acts of the Assistant Court reports the existence of 3812 pending cases. On the other hand, by official letter dated September 23, 2019, the Judge of the Second Administrative Court of the State of Baja California reports the existence of 424 active trials of the period from January 1 of the year 2000 as of December 31, 2010, as well as 5343 pending cases for the period of January 1, 2011 to date.

iii. Department of Labor and Social Welfare.

Regarding the petition 00085819 through the National Transparency Platform, the Transparency Unit of the Obligated Authority informs the pending labor law cases in the 3 Boards of Conciliation and Arbitration:

Pending labor law cases in Baja California		
Board of Conciliation	**Number**	**Observations**
Mexicali	36209	Board of Conciliation without information before 2011
Tijuana	4917	Database of 274 sheets with claimed benefits.
Ensenada	2161	Information of claimed benefits.
TOTAL	**43287**	-

As a matter of relevance, it is essential to say that the State of Baja California has pending legal cases that started before December 31, 1999, for instance, the case 81/1991, located in Clerk # 2 of the Special Board Number One of Conciliation and Arbitration of Ensenada.

iv. Baja California Attorney General.

Regarding the petition 00149119, by Off. 24/02/2019 signed by the Chief Officer of Informatics of Baja California Attorney General on February 21, 2019, and the Off. 0243/DECC/2019 dated on February 28, 2019, by the Strategy Against Crime Director of the Obligated Authority, it is informed the pending criminal cases:

TCJS			NCJS		
Temporary file	Pending	SUBTOTAL	Temporary file	Pending	SUBTOTAL
306,961	155,975	462,936	130,993	137,840	268,833

4. Baja California Sur.

i. Supreme Court of Justice of the State of Baja California Sur.

Regarding the petition 00050119, by Off. without number dated February 19, 2019, the Chief of the Transparency Unit of the Supreme Court of Justice of the State of Baja California Sur attaches an answer related to Off. CJ/DI.072/2019 signed by the Informatics Director of the Obligated Authority, were stands: *"The pending and unfinished cases cannot be obtained from databases and the judicial management system, because that information is not available in the requested period."*

Considering the content of the answer, it is promoted a claim before the State Regulator of Transparency and Access to Information because the Obligated Authority denies to reveal its judicial statistics, noting as a proof of that fact that in the National Census of State Justice Administration 2018 made by INEGI, the Supreme Court of Justice of the State of Baja California Sur did not report any information regarding pending cases.

ii. Bureaucratic Labor Court of the State of Baja California Sur.

Regarding the petition 00050319, by Off. 297/2019 dated February 21, 2019, the Administrative Coordinator of the Bureaucratic Labor Court of the State of Baja Californa Sur informs the following cases:

BUREAUCRATIC LABOR CASES (PENDING)			
Before Dec. 31, 1999	Jan. 1, 2000, to Dec. 31, 2010	Jan. 1, 2011,- Act	**TOTAL**
0	583	1643	2226

iii. Administrative Court of the State of Baja California Sur.

Regarding the petition 00068019, by Off. TJABCS/UT16/2019 dated February 13, 2019, the Transparency Unit of the Administrative Court of the State of Baja California Sur informs the content of the Off. TJABCS/SGA/095/2019 signed by the General Secretary of the Court, where mentions that, after consulting Government

Records and Judicial Statistics from June 20, 2018, to February 8, 2019, there were received 76 cases of administrative trials (74) and one administrative responsibility case (1), noting one file where was declared non-jurisdiction. Moreover, the Obligated Authority informs that there were concluded 8 cases **(10.53%),** and the litigation economic amount against the State Budget is $22,865,985.64.

iv. Board of Conciliation and Arbitration of the State of Baja California Sur.

On March 4, 2019, a claim was promoted before the State Regulator of Transparency and Access to Information because the authority denies the petition 00050019 by an obstructive algorithm in the National Transparency Platform, without any attached answer, as follows:

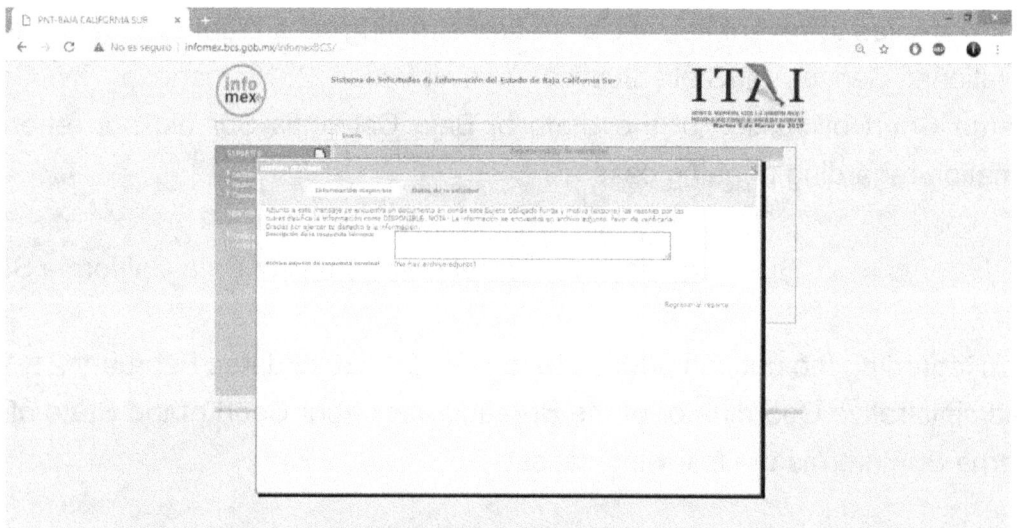

FIGURE 6. SCREENSHOT INFOMEX BCS SOFTWARE.

However, closing second edition of this book, the appeal was still pending.

v. Baja California Sur Attorney General.

Regarding petitions 00095019 and 00095119, by Off. SADAI / 291/2019 dated March 15, 2019, the Deputy Attorney General for Attention to High Impact Crimes informs of the existence of the following pending criminal cases:

TCJS			NCJS		
Temporary file	Pending cases	SUBTOTAL	Reserve	Pending cases	SUBTOTAL
4088	128	4216	15486	11257	26743

5. Campeche.

    i. Board of Conciliation and Arbitration of the State of Campeche.

Regarding the petition 0100065819, by Resolution dated February 15, 2019, the Responsible of the Unit of Access to Public Information of the Board of Conciliation and Arbitration informs the existence of the following pending cases:

PENDING LABOR LAW CASES			
Before Dec. 31, 1999	Jan. 1, 2000, to Dec. 31, 2010	Jan. 1, 2011,- Act	**TOTAL**
93	1698	2511	4302

Moreover, the Obligated Authority reveals that *"The ADRLC may vary depending on the beginning of the claim, the number of defendants, the distance of the places to notify, the type of conflict, depending on whether the parties comply with the requirements that are made by the labor authority, the amount of evidence presented by the parties to relieve, if they present an incident that indicates the article 762 of the Federal Labor Act, therefore, it can not be disclosed about the duration of the Labor judgment".*

    ii. Supreme Court of Justice of the State of Campeche.

Regarding the petition 0100065919, by Resolution 22/UT/18-2019 dated February 14, 2019, the Area Chief "A" in functions of the Unit Transparency Coordinator of the Supreme Court of Justice of the State of Campeche informs the Off. 033/DIE/18-2019, by saying:

"... In this regard, I would like to point out that in accordance with Article 216 clauses VII and IX of the General Internal Regulation of the Judicial Power of the State of Campeche, the following are general functions of this Bureau: requesting, concentrating,

processing, analyzing, systematizing and interpreting the statistical information technically that the judicial and administrative bodies generate as a result of their activities, as well as verifying that said reports comply with the requirements of truthfulness, accuracy and good faith.

However, in the statistical data capture system currently validated by this Bureau, we only have a restrictive record of quantitative movement of workloads between the number of cases initiated disaggregated according to the action or crime for which it is filed or consigned, the general number of cases in process at the end of each judicial period and number of proceedings dismissed classified by the cause of conclusion, without being part of the functions of this Directorate collecting or concentrating qualitative data of the figures reported by the courts (as to number of the file, quantum of the claimed benefits, etc.), as well as the duration of each particular process. This is in accordance with the provisions of articles 20, clause XXIV, 54, clauses II and III, 70, clause V, and article 74, clause XXVIII of the Organic Judicial Branch of the State of Campeche Act, as well as the article 109, clause VIII, letter e) of the General Interior of the Judicial Branch of the State of Campeche Regulation, which establishes the obligatory nature of the data contained in the registry books and control systems that must be generated by the courts, as well as the purpose of the statistical reports collected.

Therefore, since the information requested is not generated, processed or systematized in this administrative address to be provided in the terms required by the applicant, in accordance with articles 131 and 133 of the Transparency and Access to Information Public of the State of Campeche Act; for the case that is of use to you, the statistics generated by the jurisdictional bodies of the Judicial Branch of the State are available, which can be consulted at the electronic address http://poderjudicialcampeche.gob.mx/transparencia/, clicking in "STATISTICS" that is on the left margin of the page."

As a matter of interest, it is essential to say that Judicial Statistics of the Courts of the State of Campeche have a sophisticated disaggregation degree in the Annual Labor Report attached to, similarly as the Supreme Court of Justice of the State of Morelos.

iii. Administrative Court of the State of Campeche.

Regarding the petition 0100066019, by Off. TJA/UT/012/2019 dated February 8, 2019, signed by the Chief of the Transparency Unit of the Administrative Court of the State of Campeche, the authority informs that, from the date that the Administrative Court started, these are the following cases they have:

ADMINISTRATIVE LAW CASES		
ADMINISTRATIVE COURT OF THE STATE OF CAMPECHE		
Court	Received	Pending
Unitary Administrative Court	108	67
Unitary Specialized Court**	12	12
TOTAL	120	79
** Considers ANTI-CORRUPTION cases since January 2019.		

Moreover, the Obligated Authority reveals that the *ADRLC* is between 6 to 18 months, and, by the article 49, of the Administrative Trial Code of the State of Campeche, there are 10 days to resolve.

iv. Campeche Attorney General.

Regarting the petition 0100115919, by resolution of the Head of the Transparency Unit of the Attorney General of the State of Campeche dated March 25, 2019, the following information is available:

Estatus de los procedimientos derivados de las Carpetas de Investigación iniciadas en 2017	Corte al 31/Diciembre/2018
Determinados en archivo temporal	215
En trámite en la etapa de investigación (antes	91

Estatus de los procedimientos derivados de las Carpetas de Investigación iniciadas en 2018	Corte al 31/Diciembre/2018
Determinados en archivo temporal	246
En trámite en la etapa de investigación (antes del auto de vinculación a proceso)	1,069

6. Mexico City.

i. Judiciary Council of Mexico City.

Regarding the petition 6001000008019, by Off. CJCDMX/UT/D-0139/2019 dated February 5, 2019, signed by the Director of the Transparency Unit of the Judiciary Council of Mexico City, the authority informs that it is faculty of the President of the Supreme Court of Justice of Mexico City to elaborate and to publish Judicial Statistics disaggregated by items and categories, either to inform or to follow, to control and to evaluate legal cases.

Also, it reveals that the Judiciary Council of Mexico City has the faculty to establish the transparency levels and the privileges to Access to Judicial Statistics, according to the nature and the purposes of the information.

ii. Supreme Court of Justice of Mexico City.

Regarding the petition 6000000023519, by Off. P/DUT/1125/2019 dated February 14, 2019, the Transparency Dictaminator of the Supreme Court of Justice of Mexico City delivers a statistics Data Base (EXCEL) from courts of the City, a technical document elaborated by the Statistics Bureau of the Presidency of the Court.

According to the disaggregated information dated December 31, 2018, the Obligated Authority has these pending cases:

PENDING CASES MEXICO CITY	
Courts	**Pending to December 31, 2018.**
Civil cases	172,218
Minor amount	66,694
Civil oral trials.	22,002
Family cases.	218,017
Family oral trials.	6,968
TOTAL	485,899
Source. Data Base (EXCEL) Supreme Court of Justice of Mexico City.	
** Data are available adding up the pending cases of the Data Base closing 2018.	

Moreover, the Obligated Authority reveals the *ADRLC*, by system and topic, for 2018:

ADRLC			
2018			
Topic	**Months**	**Days**	**Total Days.**
Traditional System			
Criminal law	11	15	345
Criminal Non-Serious	9	25	295
Civil law	11	14	344
Civil Minor amount	9	22	292
Family law	7	25	235
Teenage Law	9	17	287
Oral System			
Criminal Oral without resolution	1	16	46
Criminal Oral with a resolution	4	17	137
Civil Oral	5	12	162
Family oral	3	16	106
Teenage Law	3	19	109
Source: Statistics Bureau of the Presidency, information of the Courts of the Supreme Court of Justice of Mexico City.			

As a matter of interest, it is important to mention that the Obligated Authority says:

"... it is appropriate to point out that the Office of Statistics of the Presidency, the competent area in charge of consolidating the numerical information in the Judicial Branch of Mexico City, based on the provisions of article 26, Section B, of the Political Constitution of the United States of Mexico, which establishes that the State will have a National System of Statistical and Geographic Information whose data will be considered official. For the Federation, States, Federal District, and municipalities, the data contained in the System will be of mandatory use in the terms established by law.

Once again, it is pointed out that the statistical information that is provided by this H. Court, is the one that is processed according to previously established parameters and that are based on legal ordinances such as the Political Constitution of the United States of Mexico, the Organic Superior Court of Justice of the Federal District Act, as well as in the Policies and Guidelines to which the Court's Statistical Information will be subjected, through which the official statistics generated by the aforementioned Court will be designed and implemented, according to the needs own of the aforementioned entity in addition to those of society in general.

In this sense, the aforementioned Directorate of Statistics has an INVENTORY OF VARIABLES BY INFORMATION SYSTEM on its portal, which is composed of five branches of information generated by this H. Court and the Judiciary Council, both of Mexico City, and on the basis of which the collection of statistical data of said areas of information is carried out.

The Inventory can be consulted in the following link: http://www.poderjudicialcdmx.gob.mx/estadistica/inventario-de-variables-2016/

In this link you will find five icons that in turn refer to the respective inventories of variables, according to the information material; all classified by areas in which the functionality of this H. Court is disaggregated: jurisdictional bodies, support, and the administrative regions. According to these variables, the Bureau performs its task of compiling data for quantitative purposes. The variables in question are the following:

• Online Statistical Information Capture System (CLIE)

• Capture Information System of the Institute of Forensic Sciences (INCIFO)

• *Statistical Information System of the Oral Criminal Matter (SIEMP ORAL)*

• *Statistical Information System of Criminal Matters (SIEMP)*

• *Statistical Information System of the Oral Family Matter (SIEFO)*

These variables comply with the commitment of this H. Court to contribute to an open city. ".

      iii.   Mexico City Attorney General.

Regarding the petitions 0113000118619 and 0113000118519, by Off., SJPCIDH/UT/3071/19-03 dated March 19, 2019, the Transparency Unit of Mexico City Attorney General informs *"... that this administrative unit does not have the level of disaggregation requested by the petitioner ..." (Off. 400 / ADPP / 1519 / 19-02). Also, "... the S.A.P. it is integrated with the due secrecy, because the existing database in the area has fields that indicate the name of the person who appears as the complainant, the person considered offended or victim of the crime, general data of those indicted or likely responsible , as well as the data that provide information about the investigation ... Derived from those mentioned above, it is reiterated and concluded that this Administrative Unit does not have disaggregated, nor digitized the information in the terms proposed by the applicant ... "(Off. SAPD / 300 / CA / 266 / 19-02), and "... analyzed the request ... the required information does not have that disaggregation degree ..." (Off. 200 / ADP / 370 / 2019-03)".*

Notwithstanding this official response, in an interview with MILENIO media outlet after its appearance before the Plenary Session of the Congress of Mexico City, the Attorney General informed that it will constitute the Delay Unit to combat the arrears of around 270 thousand inquiries previous and 600 thousand research folders[44].

---

[44] FISCALÍA DE CDMX INICIARÁ CON CERO REZAGOS, PROMETE GODOY, Milenio, 10 de octubre del 2019, available in https://www.milenio.com/politica/congreso/fiscalia-cdmx-iniciara-rezagos-promete-ernestina-godoy

iv. Board of Conciliation and Arbitration of Mexico City.

Regarding the petition 3400000004619, by Off. JLCA/CAJI/SE-05/19 dated February 12, 2019, signed by the Assistant Manager of the Board of Conciliation and Arbitration of Mexico City, the authority informs that there are 91,634 pending labor law cases with this disaggregation:

MEXICO CITY PENDING LABOR LAW CASES			2003	587
			2002	156
2018	24754		2001	121
2017	14897		2000	98
2016	11611		1999	63
2015	8625		1998	40
2014	7545		1997	17
2013	5014		1996	26
2012	3639		1995	22
2011	2723		1994	13
2010	2402		1993	8
2009	2183		1992	2
2008	2197		1991	2
2007	2040		1987	2
2006	1389		1981	1
2005	749		1980	1
2004	707		**TOTAL**	**91634**

In addition to this disaggregated data, the Obligated Authority says that the ADRLC is three years, approximately.

v. Administrative Court of Mexico City.

Regarding the petition 3500000003919, by Off. TJACDMX/SGCD-35/2019 dated February 5, 2019, signed by the Responsible of the General Secretary of Compilation and Diffusion of the Administrative Court of Mexico City, the authority informs that, according to the Disposition Catalog of Documents of the Administrative

Court of Mexico City, the duty to proportionate information is for the last 5 years; neither (the data) has the disaggregation degree to case file, court and the litigation economic amount, nor the pending cases; revealing the pending cases in the period 2014 to 2018:

Pending cases	
Administrative Court of Mexico City	
Year	**Cases**
2014	2991
2015	3240
2016	3819
2017	5175
2018	5695
TOTAL	20920

On the other hand, according to the Judicial Statistics of the Authority[45] during 2018, the following data was found:

Procedures	Received	Trials	Start	Judgment	Resolution
Ordinary and summary trial	4761	Trials correspond to the procedures started and reported in the next pillar.	4219	4583	
Ordinary and summary trial	5136	Trials correspond to the procedures started and reported in the next pillar.	4548	5198	
Ordinary and summary trial	5251	Trials correspond to the procedures started and reported in the next pillar.	4616	4198	
TOTAL	15148	TOTAL	13383	13979	

---

[45] Available in http://www.tjacdmx.gob.mx/index.php/articulo126-menu/fracci%C3%B3n-vi-estad%C3%ADstica-judicial

Appeal	3054	Trials correspond to the procedures started and reported in the next pillar.	2963		2873
Appeal	3341	Trials correspond to the procedures started and reported in the next pillar.	3285		2379
Appeal	2336	Trials correspond to the procedures started and reported in the next pillar.	2242		2203
TOTAL	8731	-	8490		7455

Considering 2018 information, we can estimate the RICLCRE at **54.81 %** **effectiveness** (concluded cases (judgement + resolution 2018)/ (received 2018 + pending 2014 to 2017), pending 20,920 legal cases.

7. Chiapas.

i. Constitutional Court of the State of Chiapas.

Regarding the petition 00083819, by Resolution Agreement 2/2019 dated February 20, 2019, the Responsible of the Constitutional Court of the State of Chiapas informs three pending cases, TC/14/2018 (criteria contradiction), TC/16/2018 (jurisdiction conflict) and TC/22/2018 (impediment).

ii. Judiciary Council of the State of Chiapas.

Regarding the petition 00083619, by Off. DEJ/039/2019 dated February 26, 2019, the Manager of Statistics of the Judiciary Council of the State of Chiapas informs these pending cases:

PENDING CASES.						
Judiciary Council of the State of Chiapas						
Courts	**2018**	**2017**	**2016**	**2015**	**2014**	**TOTAL**
Family Law cases.	15676	9516	7593	7406	4859	45050

Civil Law cases.	9732	4011	3051	2304	2499	21597
Criminal Law cases.	548	768	559	828	966	3669
Teenage Law cases.	0	0	112	215	277	604
TOTAL	25956	14295	11315	10753	8601	70920

iii. Administrative Court of the State of Chiapas.

Regarding the petition 00128219, by Off. TJA/SGAyP/M/014/2019 dated March 1, 2019, the General Secretary of the Administrative Court of the State of Chiapas informs the following:

"Based on the Fourth Transitory Article of the Organic Act of the Administrative Court of the State of Chiapas, the administrative files or cases in first and second instance that were in process or under any circumstances in the Regional Collegiate Civil Courts and in the Constitutional Court, they should continue to be substantiated by these, until the Administrative Court is established, which began its jurisdictional functions on March 1, 2018, it is in as much as 790 files were received from the rooms, 211 at the beginning of the year 2018, 171 revision resources from the halls. Those corresponding to 2019 up to the date of the request, a total of 82 administrative litigation proceedings have been received, 1 of administrative responsibility, three appeals.

There is a total of 172 cases resolved in the Plenary of the General Chamber of this Court, from 2018 and 2019 until the date of the request. ".

According to the answer, it can be concluded that in that Administrative Court there are 911 pending legal cases, at least.

iv. Board of Conciliation and Arbitration of the State of Chiapas.

Regarding the petition 00188719, by Off. UT/014/2019 dated March 11, 2019, the Transparency Committee of the Board of Conciliation and Arbitration informs that there are 16,625 pending labor law cases and the oldest one is located in the Special Board Number Three of Conciliation and Arbitration, dated 1992.

v. Bureaucratic Labor Court of the State of Chiapas.

Regarding the petition 00083919, by Answer Agreement PJ/TTB/UT/003/2019 dated February 26, 2019, the Transparency Unit of the Bureaucratic Labor Court of the State of Chiapas informs the Off. TTB/SGA/78/2019, which content says as follows:

> "... the Court has no record of pending cases before December 31, 1999.
>
> ...
>
> ...
>
> In the period from January 1, 2000, to December 31, 2010, 6,652 labor lawsuits were received, which are processed for a resolution to the different clerks that exist in the Court; the reason why it is up to each of them to determine those that are in process and concluded.
>
> ...
>
> ...
>
> In the period from January 1, 2011, to January 31, 2019, 7,214 labor lawsuits were received, which are processed for resolution and resolution to the different clerks that exist in this Court; the reason why it is up to each of them to determine those that are in process and concluded ... ".

vi. Chiapas Attorney General.

Regarding the petition 00183619, by resolution agreement dated March 5, 2019, the Responsible of the Transparency Unit of Chiapas Attorney General reveals the following pending cases:

TCJS			NCJS		
Temporary file	Pending	Temporary file	Pending	Temporary file	TOTAL
-	11,916	11,916	14,247	11,498	25,745

It should be noted that the Obligated Authority indicates different websites of public information, especially http://www.mes-sjp.com.mx/ (NCJS Evaluation, Following and Consolidation Model).

8. Chihuahua.

i. Supreme Court of Justice of the State of Chihuahua.

Regarding the petition *015582019*, by Off. UEJ-63/2019 dated February 6, 2019, signed by the Chief of the Statistics Unit of the Supreme Court of Justice of the State of Chihuahua, the authority informs a series of Data Base (EXCEL) files containing legal cases received Civil, Commercial and Family Law disputes, between 1999 to 2018 in the whole Judicial Districts.

As a matter of interest, in the website http://www.stj.gob.mx/estadistica/index.php, the Obligated Authority has Judicial Statistics disaggregated, also graphical booklets of its jurisdictional activity.

ii. Department of Labor and Social Welfare.

Regarding the petition 015602019 by Off. SG-T/02/2019 dated February 11, 2019, General Secretary of the Board of Conciliation and Arbitration of Chihuahua City informs the following labor law pending cases:

CHIHUAHUA PENDING LABOR LAW CASES			
Before Dec. 31, 1999	Jan. 1, 2000, to Dec. 31, 2010	Jan. 1, 2011,- Act	**TOTAL**
23	3064	13197	16284

Moreover, the Obligated Authority reveals *"... it is not possible to determine the average duration of resolution of the cases submitted to this jurisdiction because it is variable depending on various factors"*.

iii. General Department of Government.

In petition 025942019, the Obligated Authority responds *"... After analyzing the content and subject matter of the petition, I would like to inform you that the request for transparency presented is not the responsibility of this Department, since it does not provide any information on the subject in our files or records; reason why you should make the request directly to the Department of the Treasury; the foregoing, because it is the public entity where the records or data required by you could be located, and through its Transparency Unit it is given a reply to it. The preceding, because dependencies above are Obligated Authorities by the Law of the matter, and directly responsible for having the data generated or custody, among which the information you request may be found ".*

iv. Chihuahua Attorney General.

Regarding the petition 024902019, by Off. FGE-4C.5 / 1/2 / 132-2019 024902019 dated March 22, 2019, the Head of the Transparency Unit of the Attorney General of the State of Chihuahua informs the following:

"The Bureau of Criminal Statistics, through Off. FGE-5C.5.1 / 4/0411/2019, provides an answer with the information available in its files, which is described below:

Investigation folders initiated of the new criminal justice system in 2018 that are pending and pending resolution, as well as those that are in reserve in the State of Chihuahua.

(a) 41,964 cases initiated in 2018 that are under Research.
(b) 15,344 cases initiated in 2018 that are in the Temporary Archive.
(c) 11,590 cases initiated in 2018 that are concluded or in the process of being concluded.

With regard to information related to research folders integrated under the traditional system scheme, the Coordination of the Traditional System Research Unit provides the following statistical information:

Traditional System Statistics

(a) Existing Prior Inquiries: 280
(b) Prior Findings in Reserve: 10,881. "

9. Coahuila.

i. Supreme Court of Justice of the State of Coahuila.

Regarding the petition 00120619, by Off. STT/167/2019 dated February 20, 2019, the Petitions and Access to Information Unit of the Supreme Court of Justice of the State of Coahuila informs the answer elaborated by General Judicial Inspector, where the pending cases are revealed as follows:

PENDING CASES COAHUILA			
DISTRICT	Before Dec 31, 1999	Jan 1, 2000, to Dec 31, 2010	Jan 1, 2011,- Act	TOTAL
Saltillo	526	2108	31666	34300
Torreon	296	1477	29476	31249
Monclova	182	783	12258	13223
Río Grande	94	425	8900	9419
Acuña	19	153	2347	2519
Sabinas	23	223	4355	4601
Parras	63	235	3015	3313
San Pedro	14	36	1222	1272
TOTAL	1217	5440	93239	99896

Source. General Judicial Inspector.

ii. Board of Conciliation and Arbitration of the State of Coahuila.

Regarding the petition 00120719, by Off. ST/UT/47/19 dated February 20, 2019, the Transparency Unit of the Department of Labor informs the following pending labor law cases:

COAHUILA LABOR LAW	
YEAR	PENDING
2018	5638
2017	4634
2016	2989
2015	2276
2014	483
2013	784
2012	562
2011	388
2010	349

2009	457
2008	170
2007	198
2006	117
2005	69
2004	36
2003	14
2002	13
2001	3
2000	2
TOTAL	19182

Moreover, the Obligated Authority says that *"...regarding the question in which he asks to know how much is the AVERAGE DURATION OF RESOLUTION OF LEGAL CASES before this jurisdiction, I comment to him that, according to the Federal Labor Act in his articles 870 to 891, it indicates the ordinary procedure, nevertheless, in some cases, it may vary due to the procedural impulse of the parties and the appeals lodged by them. "*.

iii. Administrative Court of the State of Coahuila.

Regarding the petition *00120519*, by Off. TJA/UT/25/2019 dated February 14, 2019, the Transparency Unit of the Administrative Court of the State of Coahuila informs the Official Letters coming from the First Court, the Second Cout and the Third Court of Administrative and Tax matters, and the Specialized Court of Administrative Responsibility, all from the Obligated Authority, with the following disaggregation:

PENDING ADMINISTRATIVE CASES	
ADMINISTRATIVE COURT OF THE STATE OF COAHUILA	
COURT	PENDING CASES
FIRST COURT OF ADMINISTRATIVE AND TAX MATTERS	32

SECOND COURT OF ADMINISTRATIVE AND TAX MATTERS.	81
THIRD COURT OF ADMINISTRATIVE AND TAX MATTERS.	27
SPECIALIZED COURT OF ADMINISTRATIVE RESPONSIBILITY	4
TOTAL	144

iv. Coahuila Attorney General.

On March 13, 2019, an appeal is filed before the Guarantor Agency of the Coahuilense due to the lack of response to the petition 00201119 by the obligated party. Then, by Off. FGE-UT / 377/2019 dated March 27, 2019, the Coordinator of the Transparency Unit of the Attorney General's Office of the State of Coahuila reports the existence of the following cases:

- **Fiscalía de Personas Desaparecidas:** *"... me permito remitirle y proporcionar toda la información relacionada con la que se cuenta y en la forma que se tiene capturada...*

Total de Averiguaciones Previas Penales del 2012 a Febrero del 2019. (Sistema Tradicional)	674
Total de Carpetas de Investigación del 2012 a Febrero del 2019. (Nuevo Sistema Penal)	277

REGIÓN	AVERIGUACIONES PREVIAS PENALES (SISTEMA TRADICIONAL)	CARPETAS DE INVESTIGACIÓN (NUEVO SISTEMA PENAL)
Norte I	167	74
Norte II	44	18
Carbonífera	47	16
Centro	77	50
Laguna I	188	74
Laguna II	41	4
Sureste	110	41
TOTALES	674	277

Así mismo le informo que en esta Fiscalía de Personas Desaparecidas no se encuentra ningún asunto (Averiguación Previa o Carpeta de Investigación) "Bajo Reserva", ni en el sistema tradicional ni en el nuevo sistema penal."

- **Fiscalía Especializada en Investigación de Delitos Cometidos por Agentes del Estado:** *"...Con relación a la petición formulada por ANTONIO DE J REMES DIAZ, se informa lo siguiente:*

FISCALÍA ESPECIALIZADA EN INVESTIGACIÓN DE DELITOS COMETIDOS POR AGENTES DEL ESTADO Expedientes 2012 al 03 de marzo, 2019 (Tortura-Abuso Violento de Autoridad)			
INICIADAS	TRÁMITE	CONCLUIDO	RESERVA/ARCHIVO TEMPORAL
1098	799	296	003

- Fiscalía Especializada para la Atención de Delitos Electorales: Brinda respuesta a su petición a través del siguiente cuadro informativo:

DESGLOSE DE AVERIGUACIONES PREVIAS O CARPETAS DE INVESTIGACIÓN 2012 - 2018

AÑO	INICIADAS	ARCHIVO PROVISIONAL	NO EJERCICIO DE LA ACCIÓN PENAL	EN TRÁMITE	ACUERDO DE ABSTENCIÓN
2012	2	0	0	2	0
2013	44	10	26	8	0
2014	6	2	2	2	0
2015	3	0	1	2	0
2016	1	0	1	0	0
2017	349	0	1	9	339
2018	10	0	0	1	9

- Fiscalía Especializada en Delitos por Hechos de Corrupción: "... al respecto me permito comentarle lo siguiente:

"Solicito saber cuántas averiguaciones previas del sistema tradicional de justicia penal se encuentran en trámite y pendientes de resolver."
0 carpetas

"Solicito saber cuántas averiguaciones previas del sistema tradicional de justicia penal se encuentran en la reserva."
0 carpetas

"Solicito saber cuántas carpetas de investigación del nuevo sistema de justicia penal se encuentran en trámite y pendientes de resolver, así como aquellas que se encuentren en la reserva."
En trámite 341 carpetas de investigación.
En reserva: 06 carpetas de investigación (archivo temporal)"

v. Bureaucratic Labor Court of the State of Coahuila.

Regarding the petition 00120819, by Off. TCA/PJ/UT/012/2019 dated February 20, 2019, the Transparency Unit of the Obligated Authority informs the answer elaborated by the General Judicial Inspector, revealing the pending cases in accordance to the period:

PENDING BUREAUCRATIC LABOR CASES			
Before Dec. 31, 1999	Jan. 1, 2000, to Dec. 31, 2010	Jan. 1, 2011- Act	**TOTAL**
0	5	2026	2031

10. Colima.

i. Executive Branch.

On February 19, 2019 and March 8, 2019, Review Resources related to applications 00031119 and 00067019 are filed as the obligated party fails to respond and report on the situation that the labor lawsuits are pending and pending resolution in the State of Colima; situation that, in the resolution of the review resource

150/2019 and 171/2019 is revoked and ordered to place the available information, recorded in the Off. CG / 2269/2019, the following data:

PENDING LABOR LAW CASES	
LABOR COURT	CASES
TECOMAN	216
MANZANILLO	1513
TOTAL	1729

On the other hand, in Off. 25/2019, dated April 8, 2019, the President of the Local Conciliation and Arbitration Board of the State of Colima reports the following:

"Point number 1: In reference to this point it is necessary to point out that the information requested concerns a broad universe that refers to the State of Colima, so this answer is limited to the issues that are carried out in this Local Board of Conciliation and Arbitration of Colima, which is what concerns us, for which it is reported that derived from the information requested to the Secretariats of Agreements and the Office of the Parties of this agency, it was obtained that the trials that are pending and pending resolution 2,154, said information was obtained from the databases in the aforementioned areas. Said information is made available for your consultation and you will be personally attended at the offices located at Av. Tecomán Number 673, Colonia Luis Donaldo Colosio in Colima, Colima.

...

...

It is for the above, that the response that was delivered at the time, referring to the Conciliation and Arbitration Board of Colima is attached to the present and the response provided by the Ministry of Labor and Social Welfare through official letter DIS / 64/2019 is added , in which it delivers information regarding the Manzanillo and Tecomán Boards, in which it states that:

Manzanillo:

In the Conciliation and Arbitration Board of Manzanillo, it has so far 3449 labor trials pending; and 132 pending resolution.

The oldest file that is still in dispute is number 153/199, under the responsibility of Ms. María Lilia Contreras Ramírez, First Clerk attached to that meeting.

Tecoman:
At the Tecomán Conciliation and Arbitration Board, 114 files are pending and pending resolution.

The oldest case in dispute is: 131/2011. "

ii. Judicial Branch.

Regarding the petition 00030919, by Off. UTEE/262/2019 dated March 1, 2019, the Transparency Unit of the Supreme Court of Justice of the State of Colima informs *"... in accordance with what is stated in article 5 of the Transparency and Access to Public Information of the State Act, all the information in the possession of the obliged subjects is considered a good of public character and interest and, therefore, any person it will have access to it under the terms and conditions established in the aforementioned order, excluding the special treatment that should be granted to confidential or reserved information, as the case may be. "*

Therefore, the Obligated Authority attaches ZIP files with Statistics segmented by civil and criminal courts on basic process-phase.

Now, on the website http://stjcolima.gob.mx/transparencia/#!/declaracion/30 the Judicial Statistics of the Supreme Court of Justice of the State of Colima is available in the period from 2015 to 2017, following these data:

PENDING CASES STATE OF COLIMA	
Year	Number
2015	7,383
2016	9,673
2017	8,124
TOTAL	25,180
Source. Judicial Statistics of the Supreme Court of Justice of the State of Colima.	
** Data is obtained when subtracting of the started cases the resolutions and finished from another manner.	

iii. Colima Attorney General.

On February 28, 2019, a claim is promoted before the Transparency Regulator of the State of Colima because of the denial of the Obligated Authority to answer the petition 00062019, changing the status on the National Transparency Platform as FINISHED without any evidence.

Then, in the appeal resolution 160/2019, the obligated authority informs the following:

Averiguaciones previas y Carpetas de investigación en trámite y reversa 2012 a 22 de Mayo 2019									
	2012	2013	2014	2015	2016	2017	2018	2019	Total general
AVERIGUACION PREVIA	2255	5681	4528	2137	2349	111	44	18	17123
RESERVA	2068	5488	4300	1935	1935	52	4		15782
TRAMITE	187	193	228	202	414	59	40	18	1341
CARPETA DE INVESTIGACION			1	1412	4531	10026	12841	8343	37154
INVESTIGACION INICIAL			1	1412	4531	10026	12841	8343	37154
Total general	2255	5681	4529	3549	6880	10137	12885	8361	54277

iv. Bureaucratic Labor Court of the State of Colima.

Regarding the petition 00030819, by Off. T.A.E. 257/2019 dated February 18, 2019, the Transparency Clerk of the Bureaucratic Labor Court of the State of Colima informs the following pending cases:

PENDING CASES			
Before Dec. 31, 1999	Jan. 1, 2000, to Dec. 31, 2010	Jan. 1, 2011,- Act	**TOTAL**
0	77	3053**	3130
** Considers 2847 pending cases before the Bureaucratic Court, 152 in the Collegiate Labor Organ and 54 from the Collegiate Jurisdictional Organ.			

About the Average Duration of Resolution of Legal Cases (ADRLC), the Obligated Authority pronouns as follows: *".. the ADRLC depends on the procedural impulse that each party in the trial gives. It is true that there is legislation such as the Act that governs us Federal Labor Act that establishes deadlines and times for the action of the authority, but the impulse and speed always depend on each part generated ".*

v. Administrative Court of the State of Colima.

Regarding the petition *00031019*, by Off. 01/2019 signed by the Chief of the Transparency Unit of the Administrative Court of the State of Colima, it is revealed that on July 31, 2018, the Opening Ceremony was celebrated, extinguishing the previous Court and creating the new one. Therefore, the Obligated Authority will inform from that date until now.

About this fact, the Administrative Court informs that closing 2018 there were 244 pending cases, all of administrative and tax law. The Average Duration of Resolution of Legal Cases (ADRLC) has a period from 4 to 6 months approximately of prosecution, and six months of resolution.

11. Durango.

i. Administrative Court of the State of Durango.

Regarding the petition 00048119, by Off. TJA/P/UT/003/2019 dated February 28, 2019, signed by the Chief of the Transparency Unit of the Administrative Court of the State of Durango, the authority declares its non-jurisdiction to answer the request, suggesting to ask the Supreme Court of Justice of the State of Durango.

Because of the answer, the claim was promoted before the Transparency Regulator because the Obligated Authority must have judicial statistics since its foundation.

It is important to say that the Administrative Court, in the website http://tja.durango.gob.mx/es/Historico2017, link Judicial Statistics, EXCEL files, there is a note: *this Court that resolves disputes that arise between individuals and the state and municipal public administration, pursuant to the provisions of Article 114 of the Political Constitution of the Free and Sovereign State of Durango, in relation to the 259 of the Organic Act of the Judicial Branch of the State of Durango, and 237 of the Fiscal and Administrative Justice Act, for which it is not possible to project, generate or establish in advance goals or objectives applying operative programs or instruments or indicators, that measure the jurisdictional function entrusted constitutionally. This information has never been produced in this Court so that it will be generated and published in a maximum period of one year.*

Moreover, in the website http://tja.durango.gob.mx/es/CuartoTrimestreHistorico2017, another EXCEL file, a different note says: *This jurisdictional body resolves disputes that arise between individuals and the state and municipal public administration, in accordance with the provisions of Article 114 of the Political Constitution of the Free and Sovereign State of Durango, if it has generated this information, but not organized by the manner in which it is requested in this format, so it will be held and published in a maximum period of one year".* Therefore, a claim is promoted to nullify the answer given by the authority, to reveal the real situation of the Justice Administration of that Court.

ii. Supreme Court of Justice of the State of Durango.

Regarding the petition 00048219 by Off. **UT-TSJ-PJED OFICIO 37/2019** dated March 7, 2019, the Transparency, Access to Information and Social

Communication Manager of the Obligated Authority informs several papers elaborated by the Courts of that jurisdiction.

Independently to the given information, in the Public Repository https://consultapublicamx.inai.org.mx the Obligated Authority has the following statistics according to the received cases and the concluded cases, from the period 2013-2018:

PENDING CASES DURANGO			
Year	Received Cases	Concluded cases.	Pending
2018	34,089	20,275	13,814
2017	30,278	19,754	10,524
2016	29,771	20,166	9,605
2015	30,020	19,858	10,162
2014	29,414	18,655	10,759
2013	28,452	18,914	9,538
TOTAL	182,024	117,622	64,402

Moreover, in the statistical report, the litigation amount of Commercial disputes is estimated at $818, 884,668.64.

On the other hand, closing 2018, the Statistical Report reveals the existence of 6891 pending cases before the Bureaucratic Labor Court of the State of Durango.

iii. Department of Labor and Social Welfare.

On February 22, 2019, a claim is promoted before the Transparency Regulator of the State of Durango because of the omission to answer the petition 00048319. The complaint is registered under the case number RR/59/19.

Independently to that claim, regarding the petition 00085619, by Off. 041/2019 dated March 12, 2019, the President of the State Board of Conciliation and

Arbitration informs 6,752 pending labor law cases, noting the oldest one dated in 1980.

iv. Durango Attorney General.

Regarding the petition 00080419, by Administrative Agreement dated March 13, 2019, the Manager of the Transparency Unit of the Obligated Authority informs the following pending cases:

Durango Attorney General						
TCJS			NCJS			
Temporary file	Pending	SUBTOTAL	Temporary file	Pending	SUBTOTAL	TOTAL
9346	32,378	41,724	-	-	-	41,724

v. Governor's Office.

Regarding the petition 00085519, by Administrative Agreement dated March 14, 2019, the Responsible of the Transparency Unit of the Governor's Office informs "*It is suggested that you submit your application to the Secretary of Labor and Social Welfare of the State of Durango ...*".

vi. General Department of Government.

Regarding the petition *00085419*, by Administrative Agreement dated February 27, 2019, the Chief of the Transparency Unit of the Obligated Authority expresses its non-jurisdiction, but referring to Department of Labor and Social Welfare to ask.

12. State of Mexico.

i. Department of Labor and Social Welfare.

Regarding the petition **00003/ST/IP/2019,** by Off. 204040001/011/2019 dated February 1, 2019, signed by the Responsible of the Transparency Bureau of the Department of Labor, the authority indicates that the information is not competency of the Department, but possible available at the Board of Conciliation and Arbitration of Toluca Valley and Cuautitlan Valley too, suggesting to ask those Labor Boards.

ii. Administrative Court of the State of Mexico.

Regarding the petition 00011/TRIJAEM/IP/2019, by Agreement dated March 7, 2019, the Chief of the Documentation, Diffusion and Information Unit of the Obligated Authority reveals the information given by the Regional Courts, the Supernumerary Courts, Consultation Court, and Sections, of 4828 pending cases.

iii. Bureaucratic Labor Court of the State of Mexico.

Regarding the petition 00009/TRIECA/IP/2019, by *Off.* without number uploaded directly in the SAIMEX Software, the Obligated Authority reveals the existence of 20,393 pending cases with the following disaggregation:

PENDING BUREAUCRATIC LABOR LAW CASES			
Before Dec. 31, 1999	Jan. 1, 2000, to Dec. 31, 2010	Jan. 1, 2011,- Act	**TOTAL**
2	4548	15843	20393

In respect of the ADRLC, the Bureaucratic Labor Court answers: *"...the Average Duration of Resolution of Legal Cases that are discussed in this court are not quantifiable or approximable since the cases and dispositions of the parties are very different during the procedure."*

iv. Cuautitlan-Texcoco Valley Board of Conciliation and Arbitration.

Regarding the petition 00003/JLCACT/IP/2019, by Off. without number dated March 7, 2019, the Responsible of the Information Unit of the Obligated Authority reveals the following data:

PENDING LABOR LAW CASES			
Before Dec. 31, 1999	Jan. 1, 2000, to Dec. 31, 2010	Jan. 1, 2011,- Act	**TOTAL**
70	7,349	32,015	39,434

v. Toluca Valley Board of Conciliation and Arbitration.

Regarding the petition 00006/JLCAVT/IP/2019, by Off. JLCAVT/400E12000/006/2019 dated February 19, 2019, the General Secretary of the Obligated Authority informs that there are 9,098 pending cases. Furthermore, the Authority says that: *"In this unit, there is currently no pending trial that began before December 31, 1999 "*, and*" The average duration of labor cases is two years"*.

vi. Judicial Branch of the State of Mexico.

Regarding the petition 00069/PJUDICI/IP/2019, by Off. without number dated February 22, 2019, the Chief of the Transparency Unit of the Judicial Branch of the State of Mexico gives an EXCEL file with a list of started cases in the Courts that do not have any resolution, following this disaggregation:

PENDING CASES STATE OF MEXICO	
Nov. 1, 2011, to Feb. 7, 2019	
MATTER	CASES
CIVIL LAW	223,568
FAMILY LAW	182,453
TOTAL	406,021

Moreover, the Obligated Authority informs the Average Termination Time of Trials (ATTT) revealing year and days:

Average Termination Time of Trials (ATTT)	
Nov. 1, 2011, to Dec. 31, 2018	
Source: Judicial Statistics System.	
Consultation Date: Feb 7, 2019.	
Year	Days
2011	170.71
2012	154.88
2013	143.85

2014	135.17
2015	132.08
2016	124.19
2017	88.41
2018	55.13

vii. State of Mexico Attorney General.

In response to petition 00166 / FGJ / IP / 2019, by Off. dated March 26, 2019, the Liaison Unit of the obligated party responds: "... *In this regard, this Attorney General of the State of Mexico, based on in articles 1, 4 and 163 of the Act on Transparency and Access to Public Information of the State of Mexico and Municipalities, it is informed that as informed by the Director General of Information, Planning, Programming and Evaluation, Servant Public Enabled, information regarding the procedural status of the investigation folders is not processed, so it is not possible to meet your request in the terms you require and this Institution is not obliged to process, summarize, perform calculations or conduct investigations in accordance in the interest of the applicant, as provided in article 12 of the Transparency Act invoked above, which establishes the following: "Article 12. (...) The obliged subjects will only provide the public information that is required and that works in their archives and in the state in which it is. The obligation to provide information does not include the processing of it, nor does it present it according to the interest of the applicant; they will not be obliged to generate it, summarize it, perform calculations or conduct research. "Without another particular, I reiterate the security of my distinguished consideration. A T E N T A M E N T E M. IN A. JORGE MEZHER OFFICIAL MAJOR AND HOLDER OF TRANSPARENCY UNIT YLG / LGCG.*

13. Guanajuato.

i. Executive Branch.

On February 7, 2019, it was received an email containing the answer to the petition 00216319, signed by the Manager of the Transparency Unit and Files of the Executive Branch of the State of Guanajuato.

In the Official Letter, it is informed that the Department of Government was the Obligated Authority in charge to answer the petition, finding records of pending labor law cases incorporated to a PDF 258 file sheets of records of the State Board of Conciliation and Arbitration and the Bureaucratic Labor Court of the State of Guanajuato.

The attached document reveals the following pending cases:

JURISDICTION	LABOR LAW CASES			BUREAUCRATIC LABOR LAW CASES			TOTAL
	Before Dec. 31, 1999	Jan. 1, 2000, to Dec. 31, 2010	Jan. 1, 2011-Act	Before Dec. 31, 1999	Jan. 1, 2000, to Dec. 31, 2010	Jan. 1, 2011,-Act	
Guanajuato	159	6100	31784	2	569	4591	43205

As it can be consulted, there are at least 43,205 pending cases in those Labor Courts, noting that 161 cases started before December 31, 1999, that said, 20 years waiting for a resolution of the Labor Court.

According to the attached PDF file records at February 7, 2019, the case 21/1990/TCA/CB/IND of the Bureaucratic Labor Court and the case 424/1985/E2/CA/IND of the Special Board Number Two of Conciliation and Arbitration, were 28 years pending of bureaucratic labor law resolution and 33 years pending of labor law resolution.

Finally, the Obligated Authority reveals that the Undersecretary of Labor and Social Welfare has an institutional website[46] where judicial statistics are updated in real time. Check the next Screenshot closing 2018:

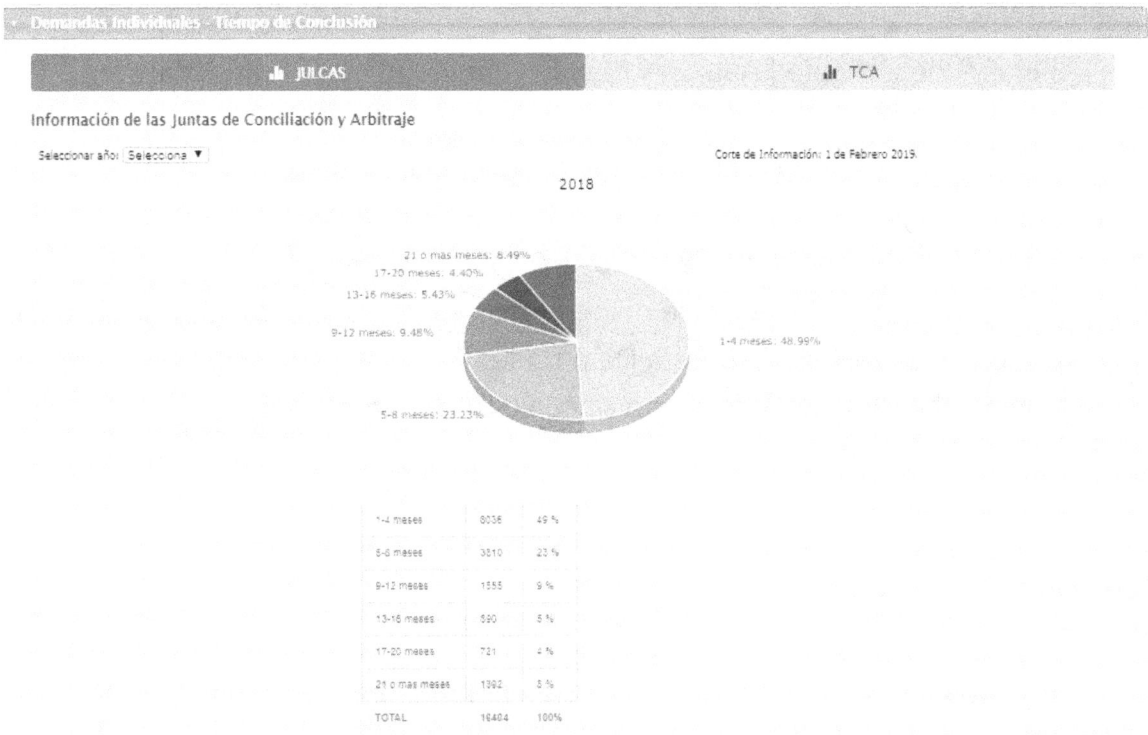

According to the disaggregated information, as we can notice, in 2018, the State of Guanajuato received 18,471 labor law cases, and 16,404 were concluded.

Considering the Real Institutional Capacity of Legal Case Resolution (RICLCRE), the Labor Board of the State of Guanajuato had **29.02% of effectiveness** (*concluded cases 2018/ received cases 2018 + pending cases 1985 to 2017*) remaining 38,043 pending labor law cases.

ii. Administrative Court of the State of Guanajuato.

Regarding the petition 00216019, by Off. UTTJA/036/2019 dated February 13, 2019, the Chief of the Transparency Unit of the Administrative Court of the State of Guanajuato informs that the cases that started before December 31, 1999, and during the period from January 1, 2000, to December 31, 2010, are concluded.

---

[46] Available in http://sg.guanajuato.gob.mx/sstps/

The cases that started in the period from January 1, 2011, to current day are 2188 (pending); the litigation economic amount cannot be revealed because it is classified information.

Finally, the Obligated Authority reveals that the ADRLC is 92.5 days.

iii. Judicial Branch of the State of Guanajuato.

Regarding the petition *00216119*, by Official Letter without number dated February 12, 2019, the Responsible of the Transparency Unit of the Judicial Branch of the State of Guanajuato delivers a Data Base (EXCEL) containing the records of Civil Courts of the State of Guanajuato since 2011 to current day; **36,936 executive commercial disputations.**

The answer emphasizes that the records are loaded in the System since 2010; therefore, it is not possible to give previous years information.

For those reasons, a motion is promoted before the Transparency Regulator of the State of Guanajuato because of the lack of information related to civil law cases, family law cases, alternative law, and criminal law cases, without underestimating the institutional capacity and efforts to reveal the full information.

iv. Guanajuato Attorney General.

Regarding the petition 00486919, by Off. 22/2019 dated March 15, 2019, the Chief of the Transparency Unit of Guanajuato Attorney General informs *"... according to our factual and legal capacity, I inform you that according to the records systematized at the date of consultation during the year 2018, we have the record of 2 TCJS cases in process and none with reserve status, as well as 58,969 NCJS cases temporary file and 9,034 in the investigation process. ".*

14. Guerrero.

    i. Guerrero Attorney General.

On March 5, 2019, a claim is promoted before the Transparency Regulator of the State of Guerrero because the Obligated Authority denies the petition 00116619 grieving the transparency regulations darkly.

Regardless of that appeal, it is important to say that in that Prosecutor's Office, at least 53,130 pending cases and 26,567 NCJS cases have been detected according to the INEGI Census, notwithstanding mentioning that during the year 2018 there were 1,851 TCJS and 21146 NCJS.

    ii. Governor's Office.

Regarding the petition 00096619 by direct answer at the National Transparency Platform, the Obligated Authority informs "... *with the aim of expediting the process, it is suggested that you direct your request to the Court of Conciliation and Arbitration of the State of Guerrero; and / or to the Department of Finance and Administration, through this way Infomex, or for more information I provide you with the following address and email: • Transparency Unit of the Ministry of Finance and Administration of the State of Guerrero. Boulevard Rene Juárez Cisneros # 130, Tepango, CP. 39095, Tel. 1160230, email: antonio.jimenez@guerrero.gob.mx Without further ado and waiting for the information to be helpful, my most cordial greeting.* ".

    iii. Supreme Court of Justice of the State of Guerrero.

Regarding the petition 00063719, by Official Letter n.19 dated March 4, 2019, the Chief of the Statistics, Evaluation and Following Unit of the Supreme Court of Justice of the State of Guerrero reveals the pending civil, criminal and family law cases:

Pending cases					
Topic	Before Dec. 31, 1999	2000-2010	2011-2018	2019	TOTAL

Criminal Law	235	23,406	4,853	-168	28,326
Civil Law	218	51,323	25,589	305	77,435
Family Law	169	49,075	56,033	842	106,119
TOTAL	622	123,804	86,475	979	211,880

iv. Administrative Court of the State of Guerrero.

Regarding the petition 00063819, by Off. 68/2019 dated March 4, 2019, the Chief Judge of the Administrative Court of the State of Guerrero informs 1588 pending administrative law cases with a litigation economic amount to the State Budget of $70, 777,299.90.

Moreover, the Chief Judge says that "...4. *The average duration of the resolutions, (how long the trials take), varies from three months to one year*".

v. Bureaucratic Labor Court of the State of Guerrero.

Closing this book edition, the petition 00167919 was still pending.

vi. Special Board of Conciliation and Arbitration of Chilpancingo.

Regarding the petition 00064019, by the direct answer in the National Transparency Platform, the Obligated Authority informs "... *Based on articles 129, 133, 134 and 135 of Number 207 Transparency and Access to Public Information of the State of Guerrero Act, this H. Special Board in the Local of Conciliation and Arbitration, cannot give this information requested since we handle records of actors who are not public officials and therefore it is private, so to be able to file it, one must have the consent of the petitioner* ".

On the other hand, Closing Spring 2019 book edition, the petition 00168119 was pending.

vii. Board of Conciliation and Arbitration of Zihuatanejo.

Regarding the petition 00168419 (Grandfathered INFOMEX Guerrero software) by Official Letter without number dated March 6, 2019, the Obligated Authority reveals:

"Regarding your request dated March 5, 2019, received before this Local Board of Conciliation and Arbitration of Zihuatanejo de Azueta, Wendy Berenice Catalan Valencia, I let you know that the undersigned is in the best disposition to comply with the various legal rules that govern us in the Mexican State, including the International Agreements ratified by our country, among which is the Transparency and Access to Public information for the State of Guerrero Act.

I express my recognition to you to be coordinating the works related to issues that will give more credibility to our institutions, for this I have to inform you that trials in process we have an approximate of three thousand records, it is said in this way because all the days are filed as totally and definitively concluded, and new demands are presented; now and in relation to his second request, that is to say, to have knowledge of the oldest judgment without ending in this Labor Organ, is the ordinary file number 129/1993 ....

I do not omit to mention that the people who make up this labor body do everything possible to comply with the provisions of the last part of Article 133 concerning Article 1 of the Political Constitution of the United States of Mexico and, therefore, prefer the human rights contained in international treaties.

Hoping to have answered your question satisfactorily, I am at your service for any problems or clarification. "

viii.   Board of Conciliation and Arbitration of Coyuca de Catalan.

Closing this book edition, the petition 00168219 was still pending.

ix. Board of Conciliation and Arbitration Number One of Acapulco de Juarez.

Regarding the petitions 00168219 and 00064219, by Off. SFA / SA / DGTyC / CSA / 008/2019 dated March 21, 2019, the System Administrator of the obligated party informs the following:

Juicios en trámite, es decir, pendientes por resolver al día de hoy: **12,472.**

Año del juicio más antiguo en trámite: **1979.**

x. Board of Conciliation and Arbitration Number Two of Acapulco de Juarez.

Regarding the petition 0016861, by Off. 1786 dated March 25, 2019, the authority informs the following:

En cumplimiento al Artículo 81 de la Ley de Transparencia y Acceso a la Información, por medio del presente me permito enviarle a Usted las Tablas de Aplicabilidad de las Obligaciones de Transparencia Comunes y Específicas de las Autoridades Administrativas y Jurisdiccionales en Materia Laboral, que rige la Segunda H. Junta Local de Conciliación y Arbitraje de Acapulco, Guerrero. La cual se adjunta al presente oficio.

xi. Board of Conciliation and Arbitration of Iguala.

Regarding the petition 00064319, by Official Letter without number directly uploaded to National Transparency Platform, the President of the Board of Conciliation and Arbitration of Iguala reveals "... *Analyzing the request points of the requested information, it is noticed that it is practically requesting information of all the labor files, however, I inform you that this H. Board has a very little legal and administrative staff, to attend the hundreds of labor lawsuits, being impossible to attend them with the required promptness within the terms established by law, given the heavy workload; therefore, the personnel in charge of collecting the information is insufficient and can not be authorized to any person given that all the staff is totally substantive to address labor issues, such as File lawsuits, bring to trial the defendants, notify agreements to both the plaintiff and the defendant, carry out the various hearings in the corresponding trials, dictate the corresponding agreements in the files, etc. Also, we have the diverse requirements of the Federal Judicial Authorities, who grant us certain places to comply with their resolutions issued in the Amparo law proceedings; hence, the impediment to obtain the information requested. However, to satisfy your request, you may appear at the address of this Board of Conciliation and Arbitration, to consult the files that are in existence, and obtain the information you mention in your request that it is about..."*

xii. Department of Labor and Social Welfare.

Regarding the petition 00064519, by Off. o UTSTyPS/022/2019 dated February 1, 2019, signed by the Chief of the Transparency Unit of the Department of Labor and Social Welfare of the State of Guerrero, related to Off. DGT/19/2019 dated March 5, 2019, signed by the General Manager of Labor and Social Welfare, the Authority says that the information is not available in the institutional records, but in the Boards of Conciliation and Arbitration of the State of Guerrero, suggesting to ask those Authorities.

15. Hidalgo.

i. Judicial Branch.

Regarding the petition 00089019, by Off. OF/UT/117/19 dated March 1, 2019, the Chief of the Transparency Unit of the Judicial Branch of the State of Hidalgo informs:

"...The information contained in the statistical systems of the Judiciary is public and can be provided to individuals in the attention to the requests for information that are presented; nevertheless, the information required by each petitioner is possible to deliver it according to the degree of disaggregation in which it is captured in the computer platforms of said systems. The information is derived from the judicial bodies of the Judicial Branch of the State of Hidalgo.

1.-Based on public utility.

2.- Fulfillment of its functions and faculties.

3.- To the extent of human, technological and institutional capabilities.

Therefore, exposed, I have to know what information you require in your application is not available.

Also, to safeguard your right of access to information, the Judiciary put it at your disposal, physical consultation, and functions conferred, at the headquarters of our institution. The information on the subject is in the direct query; however, the classified information to the Transparency and Public Information for the State of Hidalgo Act. "

    ii. Executive Branch.

Regarding the petition 00089119, by Off. dated April 3, 2019, the Transparency Unit of the Executive Branch of the State of Hidalgo reports the following:

"In order to comply with the request, in accordance with Articles 4, Section XXVI, subsections a, 24, 41, Sections I, IV and V of the Transparency and Access to Public Information for the State of Hidalgo Act, the Transparency Unit of this obligated subject is allowed to make known what is referred to by the Administrative Unit (s) responsible for the information:

1.- In response to the question asked in the sense of how many labor lawsuits that began before December 31, 1999 are pending and unfinished, it is made known that to date there is no active labor trial with the date mentioned above.

2.- In response to the question asked in the sense of how many labor lawsuits that began between January 1, 2000 and

December 31, 2010 are pending and unfinished, it is known that 83 files are found assets in the mentioned period.

In view of the file number, subject matter of judicial filing is attached file with the breakdown of the request and as for the quantum of benefits claimed this Court does not have the information in the terms requested.

FILE JANUARY 1, 2000 TO DECEMBER 31, 2010

3.- In response to the question asked in the sense of how many labor lawsuits that began between January 1, 2011 to date are pending and unfinished, it is made known that there are 1521 active files with court as of January 31 of this.

In view of the file number, subject matter of judicial filing, file is attached with the breakdown of the application and as for the quantum of benefits claimed this Court does not have the information in the terms requested.

FILE PERIOD JANUARY 1, 2011 TO DATE

4.- Regarding the average duration of resolution of issues before your jurisdiction (I ask to know how long the labor lawsuits take)

The average attention until before the award is made is two years. "

    iii. Hidalgo Attorney General.

Regarding the petition 00154319, by Off. dated April 15, 2019, the Transparency Unit of the Executive Branch reports the following:

In order to comply with the request, in accordance with Articles 4, Section XXVI, subsections a, 24, 41, Sections I, IV and V of the Transparency and Access to Public Information for the State of Hidalgo Act, the Transparency Unit of this obligated subject is allowed to make known what is referred to by the Administrative Unit (s) responsible for the information:

I request to know how many previous inquiries of the traditional criminal justice system are pending and pending resolution.

ANSWER: 14875

I request to know how many previous inquiries of the traditional criminal justice system are in reserve.

ANSWER: 15487

I request to know how many investigation folders of the new criminal justice system are in process and pending resolution, as well as those that are in the reserve.

PENDING	TEMPORARY FILE
75,668	14,328

For your interest, we are at your service".

16. Jalisco.

   i. Judiciary Council of the State of Jalisco.

Regarding the petitions *00642519* and *00748619*, by Off. 439/2019/ INCOMPETENCIA 13/ 2019 dated February 5, 2019, signed by the Transparency and Public Information Manager of the Judiciary Council of the State of Jalisco, the authority informs the partial jurisdiction between the Supreme Court of Justice of the State of Jalisco and the Alternative Justice Institute of the State.

ii. Supreme Court of Justice of the State of Jalisco.

Regarding the petition 00642019, by Off. 128/209, Inc. 24/2019 dated January 29, 2019, the Transparency Unit Chief of the Supreme Court of Justice of the State of Jalisco says that the information is not produced, generated or sheltered by that Authority, but the Judiciary Council does.

Considering the institutional delay between the Judiciary Council and the Supreme Court of Justice of the State of Jalisco, a claim is promoted before the Transparency Regulator of the State.

Later, by Off. 187/2019 dated February 12, 2019, signed by the Chief of the Transparency Unit of the Obligated Authority, the State Court reveals that *"... according to the report provided by the Department of Archive and Statistics, dependent on the Office of Comptroller, Internal Audit and Property Control of this Obligated Authority it is noted that the required information is not registered in the Statistics Data Base of the Institution, by virtue of the fact that the information is not generated in the specific form as requested by the petitioner".*

The Official Letter abounds that, *"... if it is your desire to consult the statistics of the matters resolved by the Chambers that make up this Jurisdictional Body, you can do so by entering the institutional web page, http://www.stiialisco.gob.mx, Main page, section "Transparency", Section "Fundamental", article 11, clause XIII. ".*

The authority concludes his communication by saying, *"... because of the ADRLC in this instance, is intangible because the processing of it depends on each issue."*

Contrasting the answer, in accordance to the National Census of State Justice Administration 2018, INEGI detected 2, 097,695 pending cases closing 2017 in the whole country; in Jalisco, there were 119,748 Civil, Commercial and Family Law cases, and 59,552 were concluded; therefore, **there are 60,196 pending cases at least**[47].

---

[47] Available in
https://iieg.gob.mx/contenido/SociedadGobierno/Ficha_imparticion_%20justicia_2018.pdf

However, it is true that in INEGI's Data Base *"CONJUNTO DE DATOS: IMPARTICIÓN DE JUSTICIA EN TODAS LAS MATERIAS*, pending cases[48], according to the Public Information, Jalisco indicates 0 pending cases, that is, **an omission to reveal the real pending cases.**

Now, on February 18, 2019, by Off. 777/2019 exp 89/2019 signed by the Transparency and Public Information Manager of the Judiciary Council of the State of Jalisco, the Obligated Authority delivers a Data Base (Excel) with the Judicial Statistics of the period 2000-2018.

PENDING CASES JALISCO**			
TOPIC	Period 2000-2010	Period 2011-2018	**TOTAL**
Civil Law	104240	39678	143918
Civil Law (Foreign)	76133	78333	154466
Commercial Law	113835	58266	172101
Commercial Law (Oral)	0	2850	2850
Criminal Law	29854	4716	34570
Criminal Law (Foreign)	10201	2443	12644
Mix Civil Law.	96509	57407	153916
Mix Criminal Law.	9189	-6395	2794
Family Law.	97046	110302	207348
Minor Infringers Law	0	44	44
Teenage Law	0	2631	2631
TOTAL	**537007**	**350275**	**887282**
Source. Data Base (EXCEL) Judicial Statistics of the Judiciary Council of the State Of Jalisco (2000-2018).			
**** The data is obtained by subtracting from the recorded cases the resolutions and the cases concluded by other causes.**			

---

[48] Available in https://www.inegi.org.mx/sistemas/olap/proyectos/bd/censos/gobierno2018/CNIJE2018/ImpJustTM.asp#,

From the records, the information is disaggregated by registered cases, resolutions and concluded by other causes. Taking into account the full registers and diminishing the rest of the data, then, we can obtain the following results:

As we can notice, the Data Base disaggregation proves that during the period 2000-2018 there are **887,282 pending cases**, contrasting the full information of INEGI at the National Census of State Justice Administration 2018 of **0 pending cases.**

iii. Bureaucratic Labor Court of the State of Jalisco.

Regarding the petition 00641819, by Resolution 22/2019-T dated February 11, 2019, the Chief of the Transparency Unit of the Obligated Authority attaches a Data Base (EXCEL) that contains the pending cases with the following data:

BUREAUCRATIC LABOR LAW PENDING CASES			
Before Dec. 31, 1999	Jan. 1, 2000, to Dec. 31, 2010	Jan. 1, 2011,- Act	TOTAL
5	1955	13788	15733

Now, according to the information, the oldest pending cases are 34/1994-B and 39/1994-A, where both registers indicate a disputation against the City Town of Puerto Vallarta.

Moreover, as an Obligated Authority, the Bureaucratic Labor Court of the State manages as Judicial Statistics the records of received cases[49] but denies to disaggregated the concluded ones by year.

---

[49]   Available   in   https://consultapublicamx.inai.org.mx/vut-web/?idSujetoObigadoParametro=3577&idEntidadParametro=17&idSectorParametro=30

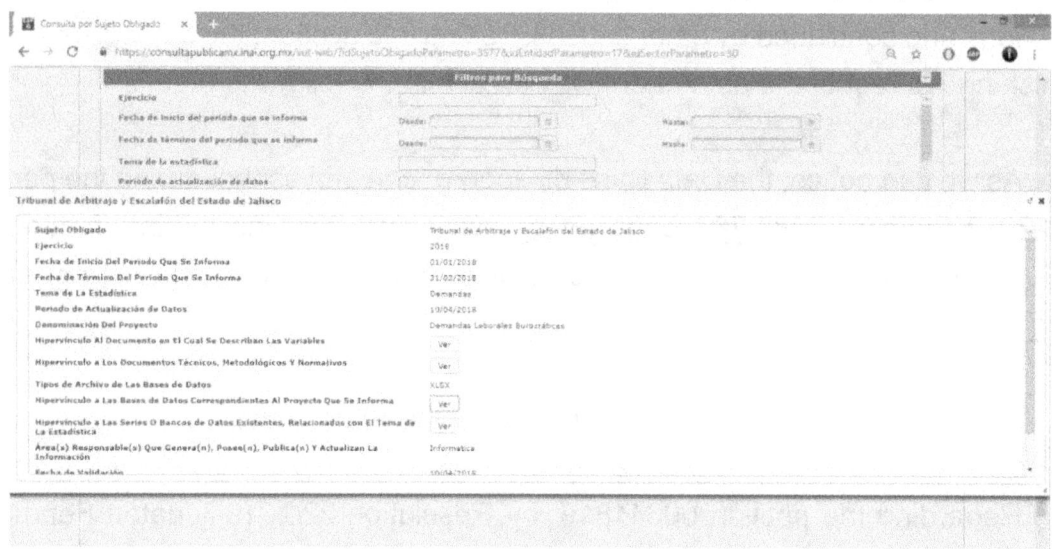

FIGURE 7. SCREENSHOT, BUREAUCRATIC LABOR COURT OF THE STATE JALISCO.

iv. Administrative Court of the State of Jalisco.

Regarding the petition *00641919*, by Off. SAIP.-051/2019-INFO dated February 11, 2019, signed by the Chief of the Transparency Unit of the Administrative Court of the State of Jalisco, the authority informs the following pending cases:

PENDING CASES		
ADMINISTRATIVE COURT OF THE STATE OF JALISCO		
Court	Pending cases to Jan. 31, 2019	Oldest case.
First Unitary Court	4240	0250/2004
Second Unitary Court	2474	0320/2008
Third Unitary Court	2473	0174/2006
Fourth Unitary Court	4164	0192/2002
Fifth Unitary Court	746	0123/2007
Sixth Unitary Court	3850	0045/2001
TOTAL	17947	-

According to Judicial Statistics[50], closing 2018, the Administrative Court of the State of Jalisco had 14,393 received cases, and 13449 were concluded, therefore, **41.59% effectiveness** (*concluded cases 2018/ received cases 2018+ pending cases 2001-2017*), and 17,947 pending cases.

v.   Department of Administration.

Regarding the petition 00719919, by Off. SECADMON/UT/253/2019 dated February 13, 2019, signed by the Chief of the Transparency Unit of the Department of Administration, the authority informs the following pending labor law cases:

Department of Administration		
Period	**Labor law cases**	**Litigation economic amount****
2000-2010	71	$17,373,418
2011-act.	332	$1,965,740,132.71
TOTAL	403	$1,983,113,551
** Disaggregated estimation in 156 legal cases.		

vi.   General Department of Government.

Regarding the petition 00720019, by Off. OAST/401-1/2019 dated January 31, 2019, the Responsible of the Transparency Unit informs the non-jurisdiction of the Obligated Authority, suggesting to The General Strategic Coordination of Economic Development of the State of Jalisco to ask the petition.

---

[50] Available in http://portal.tjajal.org/fileman/Uploads/estadi%CC%81stica%202018%20TJAJAL.pdf

vii. General Strategic Coordination of Economic Development of the State of Jalisco.

Regarding the petition 00747619, by Off. CGECDE/UT/EXPINT-021/2019 signed by the Responsible of the Transparency Unit of the Obligated Authority, the authority informs the Official Letter 61/2019 and the statistical records of the labor law cases, available in https://stps.jalisco.gob.mx/justicia-laboral/emplazamientos.

Now, it is convenient to say that the State Board of Conciliation and Arbitration has Open Data, to dispose the complete information. Therefore, Judicial Statistics is disaggregated in the period 2011 to 2018 with the following data:

PENDING LABOR LAW CASES			
YEAR	RECEIVED	CONCLUDED	PENDING CASES
2018	22343	11766	10577
2017	24509	12303	12206
2016	23278	15476	7802
2015	22694	14281	8413
2014	23772	18035	5737
2013	24086	15910	8176
2012	24408	15379	9029
2011	20462	15384	5078
TOTAL	185552	118534	67018

As we can review, closing 2018, the State of Jalisco had a RICLCRE for solving Labor Law cases of **14.93%** (*concluded cases 2018/ received cases 2018+ pending cases 2011-2017*), pending 67018 labor law cases at least.

In this case, the proposition "at least" is argued because manual records in the State Board of Conciliation and Arbitration elaborated 2010-year pending cases into the past.

Therefore, in the National Transparency Platform, a claim is promoted before the Transparency Regulator of the State of Jalisco, to reveal 2010-year and previous records. Also, a new petition (01062819) is formulated to check the documents, almanacs, and papers that will corroborate the pending labor law cases.

The petition is answered by Official Letter CGDE/DJ/UT/EXPINT-055/2019 dated February 22, 2019, where the attached documents related to the President of the State Board of Conciliation and Arbitration reveals: *"...the Local Board of Conciliation and Arbitration in the State of Jalisco does not have manual records of more than 5 years ... by the flow of the different actions the numbers constantly vary, resulting in a total of 98,000. As for the data of the oldest file dates from the year 1993. "*.

viii.   Jalisco Attorney General.

Regarding the petition 01247419, by Resolution FG/UT/2038/2019 dated March 6, 2019, the Chief of the Transparency Unit of Jalisco Attorney General informs as follows:

Jalisco Attorney General.			
System	Pending	Temporary File.	TOTAL
TCJS	18,018	77,593	95,611
NCJS	81,908	61,985	143,893
TOTAL	99,926	139,578	239,504
Source. Specific Inform of the Transparency Unit of Jalisco Attorney General.			

17. Michoacan.

i. Michoacan Attorney General.

Regarding the petition 00188519, by Off. ST-01207/2019 dated March 1, 2019; the Clerk of the Transparency Unit of Michoacan Attorney General informs the following information:

Michoacan Attorney General			
System	Pending	Suspended and Temporary File.	TOTAL
TCJS	20167	270496	290663
NTCS	25624	94156	119780
TOTAL	45791	364652	410443
Source. General Bureau of Information of Michoacan Attorney General.			

ii. Judicial Branch of the State of Michoacan.

Regarding the petition 00102919, by Official Letter dated February 20, 2019, the Chief of the Transparency Unit of the Judicial Branch of the State of Michoacan reveals the following pending Civil, Family, Commercial and Criminal Law cases:

Pending cases Judicial Branch of Michoacan.				
Topic	Before Dec. 31, 1999	Jan. 1, 2000, to Dec. 31, 2010	Jan. 1, 2011,- Act	TOTAL
Civil, Commercial and Family Law	926	2547	82756	86229
Criminal Law	646	3902	12024	16572
TOTAL	1572	6449	94780	102801

As a matter of interest, in the State of Michoacan, the oldest pending legal cases are dated from 1967 (Civil Law) and 1974 (Criminal Law, 5 cases).

iii. State Board of Conciliation and Arbitration.

Closing this book edition, the petition 00103019 was still pending.

iv. Administrative Court of the State of Michoacán.

Regarding the petition 00103119, by Off. **TJAM/UDT/025/2019** dated February 7, 2019, the Chief and Coordinator of the Transparency Unit of the Obligated Authority reveals the existence of public information available in www.tjamich.gob.mx. Therefore, according to Judicial Statistics, closing 2018, these legal cases are pending:

ADMINISTRATIVE PENDING CASES.		
ADMINISTRATIVE COURT OF THE STATE OF MICHOACAN.		
PERIOD (2018)	Received	Concluded
Jan-March	633	385
April-June	601	481
July-Sept.	347	470
Oct- December	276	414
TOTAL	1857	1750

Considering the Judicial Statistics disaggregation, it is estimated that the RICLCRE is **55.70%** (*concluded cases 2018/ received cases 2018 + pending cases 2015 to 2017*), pending 1392 cases for 2019 resolution.

v. Bureaucratic Labor Court of the State of Michoacan.

Regarding the petition 00103219, by Off. TCAEM/UT/08/2019 dated February 25, 2019, the Responsible of the Transparency Unit of the Obligated Authority informs:

"In virtue of the fact that the information requested is personal data contained in the proceedings of the files that are processed before this Court and said data are classified as restricted access information in the confidential mode, on which, it can not perform any act or act without the proper authorization of the holders or their legal representatives, this is based on Article 101 of the Transparency, Access to Public Information and Protection of Personal Data of the State of Michoacan de Ocampo Act ... therefore, the request made cannot prosper. "

18. Morelos.

i. Judiciary Council of the State of Morelos.

Regarding the petition *00085319*, by Off. dated February 5, 2019,(sealed by the General Clerk of the Supreme Court of Justice of the State of Morelos), the authority informs that the Judiciary Council of the State of Morelos was extinguished by Public Declaration published in the Official Newspaper "Tierra y Libertad" number 5578, Proclamation number 2589 that reforms several articles of the Political Constitution of the State of Morelos, the Administrative State Court Organic Act and the Attorney General Organic Act, noting the transitory articles 14th and 17th were the functions of the Obligated Authority are assumed by the Supreme Court.

Because of the answer, a claim is promoted before the Transparency Regulator of the State of Morelos, to reveal the information, in any case, until the date that the authority was extinguished.

ii. Supreme Court of Justice of the State of Morelos.

Regarding the petition *00085519*, by Official Letter without number dated February 5, 2019, the Chief of the Transparency Unit of the Obligated Authority informs that the judicial statistics are not disaggregated in accordance to the petition terms; therefore, it declares the inexistence of a specific regulation to reveal the information as the request points.

Independently to that situation, the answer indicates a duty in accordance to articles 73, clause II and 94 BIS, clause IV, from the Supreme Court of Justice of the State of Morelos Organic Act, that the Judges will send to the Higher Court in the first 5 days of each month, a report related to received and concluded cases, Furthermore, to reveal statistical records, because of the obligation of the Bureau Administrator of the Courts, to send to the Chief Justice of the Supreme Court both, a monthly and yearly report of the cases each Court has.

The answer indicates that in the web site http://tsjmorelos2.gob.mx/ section INSTITUTION, subsection LABOR REPORT, there are the public accountability papers since 2009 until now, with judicial statistics. However, the information is not ordered and without disaggregation.

Finally, the Obligated Authority argues that the petition is an *ad-hoc* motion; therefore, it cannot reveal the information.

Considering these facts, on February 7, 2019, a claim is promoted before the Transparency Regulator of the State of Morelos, so that the Obligated Authority might reveal its statistical records and disaggregated petitions points.

iii. Administrative Court of the State of Morelos.

Regarding the petition 00085419, by Official Letter without number directly uploaded to the National Transparency Platform- INFOMEX, the Transparency Unit of the obligated authority reveals: "... *this jurisdictional authority informs the applicant that the information required is not feasible to produce it and, if applicable, deliver it in the form in which it is requested, since the handing over of the information by this Court does not imply prosecution or the adequacy of the same to the interest of the applicant. Reiterating that the information produced, published and updated by this Administrative Court of the State of Morelos following the Transparency and Access to Public Information of the State of Morelos Act, can be found in the electronic link indicated above.* "

iv. Unitary Teenage Court of the State of Morelos.

By Official Letter without number dated February 15, 2019, the Obligated Authority informs *"... I would like to request from you, the extension established in the provisions of article 103 of the Transparency and Access to Public Information of the State of Morelos Act, the aforementioned, because the information requested was changed to different areas of this Court to be able to collect it and be able to respond to your request. "*.

v. Morelos Attorney General.

Regarding the petition 00151419, by Off. DGIyPPFRM/472/2019-02 dated February 21, 2019, the General Manager of Investigation and Criminal Prosecution of the Attorney General informs that *"... because the Official Letter does not provide temporary work it is not possible to answer your request".*

Because of the answer, a claim is promoted before the Transparency Regulator of the State of Morelos.

vi. Department of Labor- Board of Conciliation and Arbitration of the State of Morelos.

Regarding the petition *00085719*, by Off. JLCA/170/19 dated February 12, 2019, the President of the Board of Conciliation and Arbitration of the State of Morelos informs the following labor law pending cases:

LABOR LAW CASES			2010	1375
2001 AND PREVIOUS	240		2011	1623
2002	179		2012	2290
2003	226		2013	2519
2004	292		2014	2343
2005	201		2015	1967
2006	424		2016	2248
2007	655		2017	2634
2008	672		2018	2806
2009	713		2019	296
			TOTAL	23703

Having exposed the pending cases, the President of the Board of Conciliation and Arbitration says that the ADRLC, while is true that 2012 Federal Labor Act establishes that the trial time will be 1 year, it is also true that there is a lack of human and legal resources to accomplish the regulations on time; therefore, the ADRLC is variable.

19. Nayarit.

i. Executive Bureau.

Regarding the petition 00066419, by Off. DE/UT/016/2019 dated February 18, 2019; the Chief of the Transparency Unit of the Executive Bureau expresses its non-jurisdiction to answer the petition, suggesting the General Department of Government.

ii. Administrative Court of the State of Nayarit.

Regarding the petition 00037319, by Official Letter without number directly uploaded in the grandfathered INFOMEX software, the General Clerk of the Obligated Authority informs:

"I request to know how many trials that began between January 1, 2000, and December 31, 2010, are in process and without concluding. R. 2 (two)
I request to know file number, N / A
The subject, Administrative R.
Judicial filing body, R. Administrative Court of Justice
Quantum of claimed benefits. N / D

- I request to know how many trials that began between January 1, 2011, to date, are in process and not concluded. R.600 (six hundred)
I request to know file number, N / A
The subject, Administrative R.
Judicial filing body,
 R. Administrative Court of Justice
Quantum of claimed benefits. N / D

...

The Justice and Administrative Procedures of the State of Nayarit Code and its regulations do not indicate any term or term to resolve administrative trials, since within the same proceedings there are recourse and incidents to be processed, which by their nature suspend the procedure, there is also the right of the defendant to appeal to federal justice through the direct or indirect Amparo trial, which establishes their terms".

iii. Judicial Branch.

The petitions 00037419 and 00133719 were formulated before the National Transparency Platform to reveal the situation of the Judicial Branch of the State of Nayarit.

Independently to that fact, according to the Judicial Statistics of the Obligated Authority[51], it can be consulted the Statistics Report 2017, closing 2017, there were 36,810 pending cases.

iv. Department of Labor, Productivity and Economic Development.

On March 13, 2019, two claims are promoted before the Transparency Regulator of the State because the Obligated Authority, in the petitions 00066319 and 00037519, demands the payments of fees to reveal the information. Besides, closing thisbook edition, the petition 00133619 was still pending.

v. Nayarit Attorney General.

Closing this book edition, the petition 00075419 was still pending.

vi. Administrative Court of the State of Nayarit.

Closing this book edition, the petition 00037319 was still pending.

---

[51] Available in http://www.tsjnay.gob.mx/transparencia/fraccion-xxx-estadisticas/

20. Nuevo Leon.

i. Supreme Court of Justice of the State of Nuevo Leon and Judiciary Council.

Regarding the petitions **140819** and **141219,** by Resolution dated February 13, 2019, the Legal Manager and Responsible of Information of the Judiciary Council of the State of Nuevo Leon informs: *"... In light of the fact that the request made by the applicant is about direct questions of a statistical nature, it is essential to inform that the right of access to information refers to the obtaining of documents that the obliged authority has under his protection as well as has generated, and not to get specific opinions or pronouncements, nor for the request for the generation of instruments that meet particular needs, as in the particular case.*

For this instrument could only be the product of a search and a discarding of information in the entire universe of files that the Judiciary is in charge of; activity that is not specific to the exercise of the right of access to information, since there is no regulation that would lead you to informally generate the classification of information in the way you request it.

Therefore, it is clear from the previous that it prepared a petition that is consecrated under the fundamental right provided for in article 8 of the Political Constitution of the Free and Sovereign State of Nuevo León, and not under the article 6 that refers to the right of access to information.

In such conditions, the processing of their information requirement was aired in the light of the exercise of the fundamental right of Petition, established in Article 8 of the Constitution, and not through the use of the fundamental right of Access to Information. "

Independently to the content of the answer, the obligated authority says that the Judicial Statistics Office has not available information to communicate, but informs about the ADRLC, as follows:

Materia	Cant.de dias
civiles	175
concurrentes	239
menores	99
familiar	146
oral.familiar	47
oral.civil	118
oral.mercantil	133
virtual.familiar	7
mixtos	128

Finally, the Obligated Authority reports the existence of the website https://www.pjenl.gob.mx/Estadistica/ where the judicial statistics reveal the following data:

LA JUSTICIA EN NÚMEROS

Cantidades acumulativas del 1 de enero al día último del mes registrado.

2018   2017

Concepto	Ene	Feb	Mar	Abr	May	Jun	Jul	Ago	Sep	Oct	Nov	Dic
Número de Magistrados	15	15	14	14	14	14	14	14	14	14	14	
Número de Jueces	122	122	120	123	121	121	121	122	122	125	125	
Audiencias Orales	4,560	9,995	14,832	20,453	26,559	32,432	36,614	43,887	49,522	56,024	62,679	
Asuntos Recibidos	13,189	26,568	37,959	53,901	69,277	84,006	95,820	112,972	127,081	143,051	157,396	
Asuntos en Trámite	67,615	67,508	67,472	67,734	67,616	67,066	68,900	69,405	69,442	68,356	68,129	
Asuntos Resueltos	14,263	27,777	39,228	54,911	70,302	85,584	95,552	112,303	126,382	143,463	158,032	

FIGURE 8. JUDICIAL STATISTICS DISAGGREGATION OF THE JUDICIAL BRANCH OF NUEVO LEON.

As we can appreciate, the Judicial Branch of the State of Nuevo Leon has disaggregated information that reveals the RICLCRE closing 2018 of **69.59 %** (*Concluded cases 2018/ Received cases 2018 + pending cases 2018),* with 68,129 pending cases.

ii. Board of Conciliation and Arbitration of the State of Nuevo Leon.

Regarding the petition 00140919, by Agreement dated February 21, 2019, the General Clerk "C" and Responsible of Transparency Unit of the Obligated Authority informs the following pending labor law cases:

PENDING LABOR LAW CASES.			
Before Dec. 31, 1999	Jan. 1, 2000, to Dec. 31, 2010	Jan. 1, 2011,- Act	TOTAL
0	13	8608	8621

Moreover, the Obligated Authority informs *"The duration is very varied in each particular case. In the particular case of the period of information required and taking into account the number of trials, the time in which each of them was resolved and the date of its conclusion, an average time of approximately 8.05 months is obtained ... ",* attaching the following ADRLC data:

Promedio anual de la duración de juicios			
año	promedio en días	promedio en meses	promedio en años
1998	102	3.4	0.279452055
1999	112	3.733333333	0.306849315
2000	156	5.2	0.42739726
2001	221	7.366666667	0.605479452
2002	250	8.333333333	0.684931507
2003	263	8.766666667	0.720547945
2004	315	10.5	0.863013699
2005	389	12.96666667	1.065753425
2006	347	11.56666667	0.950684932
2007	337	11.23333333	0.923287671
2008	343	11.43333333	0.939726027
2009	370	12.33333333	1.01369863

2010	345	11.5	0.945205479
2011	318	10.6	0.871232877
2012	304	10.13333333	0.832876712
2013	308	10.26666667	0.843835616
2014	271	9.033333333	0.742465753
2015	190	6.333333333	0.520547945
2016	152	5.066666667	0.416438356
2017	131	4.366666667	0.35890411
2018	86	2.866666667	0.235616438
2019	11	0.366666667	0.030136986

iii. Administrative State Court of Nuevo Leon.

On February 22, 2019, a claim is promoted before the Transparency Regulator of the State of Nuevo Leon because the Obligated Authority sets FINISHED the petition 00141019 in the National Transparency Platform without an answer and attached document.

Therefore, on appeal RRA 39/2019, the obligated authority informs the following:

Los juicios que se encuentran en trámite son a partir del año 2010 a la fecha, y de los cuales se obtuvo las siguientes cantidades:

Año	Juicios en trámite y sin concluir.
2010	7
2011	27
2012	32
2013	29
2014	56
2015	103
2016	404
2017	695
2018	1008
2019	410

iv. Bureaucratic Labor Court of the State of Nuevo Leon.

On February 22, 2019, a claim is promoted before the Transparency Regulator of the State of Nuevo Leon because the Obligated Authority sets FINISHED the petition 00141119 in the National Transparency Platform without an answer and attached document.

In that sense, in the appeal 38/2019, the AUTHORITY reports the existence of 431 bureaucratic pending cases.

v. Nuevo Leon Attorney General.

Regarding the petition 00213819, by Off. FGJ/DTAIYAJ/366/2019 dated March 4, 2019, the Transparency Manager of the Obligated Authority informs the following pending criminal cases:

Nuevo Leon Attorney General.				
System	Procedure	Pending	Reserve	TOTAL
TCJS	7,944	505,604	380,769	894,317
NCJS	154,022	213,495	0	367,517
TOTAL	161,966	719,099	380,769	1,261,834

Also, according to the NCJS Evaluation, Following and Consolidation Model (available in http://www.mes-sjp.com.mx/) we find that, among the years 2017-2018, Nuevo Leon had 43,806 criminal cases in the Temporary File (32,136 and 11,670).

21. Oaxaca.

i. Board of Agrarian Conciliation of the State of Oaxaca.

On February 8, 2019, a claim is promoted before the Transparency Regulator of the State of Nuevo Leon because the obligated authority sets in the National Transparency Platform the status ANSWERED and NONEXISTENT

INFORMATION, but the authority does not attach either Official Letter or Documents. The claim is registered with the number R.R.A.I. 0043/2019.

Independently to the denial, through grandfathered INFOMEX Oaxaca software, the answer is uploaded in the Off. JCA/226/2019, revealing: *"... does not have such information since by articles 12 and 14 of this unit only has conciliatory functions in land disputes between ejidos, agrarian communities, and small owners.".*

ii. Board of Conciliation and Arbitration of the State.

On February 26, 2019, a claim is promoted before the Transparency Regulator of the State of Oaxaca because the obligated authority denies answering the petition 00073519. Moreover, closing spring 2019 book edition, request 00142719 was pending.

Then, on petition 00142719, the obligated authority informs the following:

Se entiende que en trámite se refiere del inicio de la demanda hasta la formulación de alegatos y pendientes de resolver los que se encuentran en laudo por lo anterior se contesta que hay 7616 expedientes activos en la Junta de los cuales 5616 se encuentran en trámite y 2000 pendientes de resolver y el expediente activo más antiguo es del año 1981 en situación de trámite y del año 1992 en situación pendiente de resolver.

Esperando que la respuesta sea satisfactoria queda esta autoridad a su disposición.

iii. Supreme Court of Justice of the State of Oaxaca.

Regarding the petition 00073719, by Off., PJEO/CJ/DPI/UT/00.01.01./219/2019 dated March 12, 2019, the Responsible of the Transparency Unit of the Supreme Court of Justice of the State of Oaxaca informs: *"...the documents for direct consultation are made available to the applicant ...".* Likewise, the obliged authority says: *"You can not establish a time for a trial since everything depends on the impulse and speed that the parties give to."*

iv. Administrative Court of the State of Oaxaca.

Regarding the petition 00073819, by Off. TJAO/UT/19/2019 dated March 6, 2019, the General Clerk of the Administrative Court of the State of Oaxaca informs the following pending cases (from 2016 to 2019):

PENDING CASES	
ADMINISTRATIVE COURT OF THE STATE OF OAXACA	
Topic	**number**
Administrative cases 2016	1427
Unconformity cases 2016	5
Administrative cases 2017	734
Unconformity cases 2017	8
Administrative cases 2018	834
Unconformity cases 2018	5
Administrative cases 2019	55
Unconformity cases 2019	0
TOTAL	**3068**

Moreover, the Obligated Authority reveals "*... the duration of the trials is very variable, because within the procedural stage of the trials, there are some tests that need more time to be relieved, also at the compliance stage by the defendant authority is totally dependent on the willingness of said authorities to comply with the judgments, with the understanding that the trial cannot be concluded without first satisfying the plaintiff's claim. However, in matters in which the authority complies in time and form with the request of the actor, the trials last for five months in some and others that go up to twelve months. *".

v. Bureaucratic Board of the State of Oaxaca.

Regarding the petition 00073919, by Off. without number dated February 20, 2019, the Chief of the Transparency Unit of the Obligated Authority informs the following pending cases:

BUREAUCRATIC LABOR LAW PENDING CASES			
Before Dec. 31, 1999	Jan. 1, 2000, to Dec. 31, 2010	Jan. 1, 2011,- Act	**TOTAL**
5	20	816	841

vi.   Oaxaca Attorney General.

Regarding the petition 00122019, by Off. FGEO/DAJ/U.T./561/2019 dated March 9, 2019, the Legal Manager and Responsible of the Transparency Unit of the Obligated Authority informs the following pending cases:

Oaxaca Attorney General			
System	**Pending**	**Reserve**	**TOTAL**
TCJS	180,276	12,831	**193,107**
NCJS	55,472	3,136	**58,608**
TOTAL	**235,748**	**15,967**	**251,715**

22. Puebla.

i.   Judicial Branch of the State of Puebla.

Regarding the petition 00148019, by Off. UTPJ/195/2019 dated February 25, 2019, the Chief of the Transparency Unit of the Judicial Branch of the State of Puebla informs: *"According to the statistical report submitted by the courts, the number of trials pending resolution is not recorded, only the number of files filed is available, as well as the number of judgments handed down, which is attached to this."*. Then, the obligated authority gives a list of 2018 resolutions of Civil, Family, Commercial and Criminal Law legal cases.

Independently to the revealed information, through Judicial Statistics of the State of Puebla[52], the following data are disaggregated:

---

[52]   Available   in   http://www.htsjpuebla.gob.mx/secciones/estadisticas/   and https://consultapublicamx.inai.org.mx/vut-web/?idSujetoObigadoParametro=3577&idEntidadParametro=17&idSectorParametro=30

Judicial Branch of the State of Puebla			
Year	Cases	Resolutions	Pending
2018	49,809	27883	21,926
2017 **	-	-	-
2016**	-	-	-
2015	60,155	46,704	13,451
2014**	-	-	-
2013	61,726	34,843	26,883
2012	58,326	32,935	25,391
2011	65,295	36,441	28,854
2010	64,812	38,010	26,802
2009	70,636	39,393	31,243
2008	72,324	39,346	32,978
2007	67,880	36,076	31,804
2006	64,781	34,329	30,452
2005	56,411	31,805	24,606
2004	72,723	39,109	33,614
2003	74,295	37,383	36,912
2002	67,049	34,837	32,212
2001	63,995	34,811	29,184
2000	60,433	32,368	28,065
TOTAL	1,030,650	576,273	454,377

Source. Evaluation and Control Department of the Judicial Branch, available in http://www.htsjpuebla.gob.mx/secciones/estadisticas/index.php

*** According to Judicial Statistics, it cannot obtain the number of received and concluded cases.*

ii. Administrative Court of the State of Puebla.

Regarding the petition 00110219, by Off. without number dated February 20, 2019, the Transparency Unit of the Administrative Court of the State of Puebla reveals about 346 pending legal cases, with a litigation economic amount charged to the State Budget of $218, 854,341.70 (at least).

iii. Board of Conciliation and Arbitration of the State of Puebla.

Regarding the petition 00110419, the Transparency Unit of the Obligated Authority informs directly in the grandfathered INFOMEX software "... *There are fourteen lawsuits in process within the referred period ... It is reported that there are 3149 lawsuits in process, within the period above ... Respect for the information requested, there are 11711 lawsuits in the process, within the referred period ...*".

iv. Puebla Attorney General.

Regarding the petition 00202719, by Off. dated March 21, 2019, the Transparency Unit of the Attorney General of the State of Puebla informs the following:

CONCEPTO	EN TRÁMITE	ARCHIVO TEMPORAL
AVERIGUACIONES PREVIAS	2,670	N/A
CARPETAS DE INVESTIGACIÓN	85,559	N/A

Nota: la leyenda N/A se refiere a información que no cuenta con el desglose solicitado.

23. Queretaro.

i. Judicial Branch of the State of Queretaro.

Regarding the petition 00065619, by Off. UT/056/2019 dated February 19, 2019, the Chief of the Transparency Unit of the Judicial Branch of the State of Queretaro informs "... *the requested data are available publicly and without any restriction ...*", abounding in the sense of "... *are part of public records or public access sources, such as print media, or, on the Internet portal, relative to the National Institute of Statistics and Geography (INEGI) ... the result of judicial statistics data issued by this and by other Judicial Branches of the country related to the delivery of justice ... ".*

ii. Bureaucratic Labor Court of the State of Queretaro.

Closing this book edition, the petition 00065719 was still pending.

iii. Administrative Court of the State of Queretaro.

By Official Letter OM/077/2019 dated February 28, 2019, the Chief of the Transparency Unit of the Obligated Authority answers the petition 00065819 by saying *"... I inform you that we only have information from the Administrative Court of the State of Querétaro, from the year 2017 to the date."*

According to its Judicial Statistics in 2018[53], the Administrative Court of the State of Queretaro had 1675 in process and 252 pending cases of resolution.

iv. Executive Branch.

By Official Letter SPF/UTPE/SASS/286/2019 dated February 27, 2019, the petition 00065919 is answered as follows:

- Se encuentran 12 demandas que comenzaron antes del 31 de diciembre de 1999 con estatus Vigente, todos de materia Laboral y lo que refiere al quantum de prestaciones reclamadas, en el sistema no hay un campo que especifique este dato, tendría que consultarlo en la Junta Especial correspondiente. Detalle en Pág.2
- Se encuentran 1,201 demandas entre el 1 de enero del año 2000 al 31 de diciembre del año 2010 con estatus vigente, todos en materia laboral, y lo que refiere al quantum de prestaciones reclamadas, en el sistema no hay un campo que especifique este dato, tendría que consultarlo en la Junta Especial correspondiente. Detalle en Págs.2-32
- Se encuentran 25,736 demandas que comenzaron entre el 1 de enero del año 2011 a la fecha, con estatus vigente, todos de materia Laboral y lo que refiere al quantum de prestaciones reclamadas, en el sistema no hay un campo que especifique este dato, tendría que consultarlo en la Junta Especial correspondiente. Págs. 33-676

---

[53] Available in http://queretarotca.com/tca2/transparencia/estadistica/Juzgados2018.pdf

v. Queretaro Attorney General.

Regarding the petition 00110319, by Off. Dated april 2 2019, the obligated autorithy informs the following:

EN RESPUESTA: Por cuanto ve al primer punto de su solicitud, el número de reservas que se informan son aquellas que se dieron del 30 de mayo de 2016 al 28 de febrero de 2019.

Trámite	Reserva
459	5789

Respecto al segundo punto de su solicitud, las cifras corresponden a las que se iniciaron del 01 de enero al 28 de febrero de 2019, por cuanto ve a las determinaciones son aquellas que fueron determinadas en el mes de enero y febrero de 2019.

Inicios	Determinaciones	Archivos temporales	Trámite
9631	2211	5311	7420

24. Quintana Roo.

i. Quintana Roo Attorney General.

Regarding the petition 00175119, by Off. FGE/DFG/UT/INFO/586/2019, F: 108/2019, the Chief of the Transparency Unit of Quintana Roo Attorney General informs the following criminal cases:

Quintana Roo Attorney General				
System	In process	Pending	Reserve	TOTAL
TCJS	88,890	102	6,592	95,584
NCJS	7,333	5,985	570	13,888
TOTAL	96,223	6,087	7,162	109,472

ii. Judicial Branch of the State of Quintana Roo.

Regarding the petition 00117619, by Off. UT/RS/039/2019 dated March 7, 2019, the Chief of the Transparency Unit of the Obligated Authority reveals the following pending cases:

Pending cases				
Topic	Before Dec. 31 1999	Jan. 1 2000 to Dec. 31 2010	Jan. 1 2011- Act	TOTAL
Family Law	138	923	13,537	14,598
Civil Law	1509	6,030	8,078	15,617
Commercial Law	0	798	7,854	8,652
Criminal Law	0	51	1,431	1,482
TOTAL	1647	7,802	30,900	40,349

Furthermore, the Obligated Authority informs that the ADRLC is: *From 2 to 4 years in family cases, from 1 year to 3 years in commercial disputes, from 4 to 6 months in civil proceedings, an average of 6 months to 2 years in criminal cases."*

iii. Administrative Court of the State of Quintana Roo

Regarding the petition *00117719*, by Off. TJA/UT/027/2019 dated February 15, 2019, the Chief of the Transparency Unit of the Administrative Court of the State of Quintana Roo says that it has available information since the foundation of the Court in 2018. Therefore, the Clerks of each of the Unitary Courts reveal the ADRLC available data, as follows:

ADRLC	
Administrative Court of the State of Quintana Roo.	
Court	Time
1st Court	160.2 days
2nd Court	161.4 days
3rd Court	7.5 months
4th Court	106.5 days

iv. Department of Labor and Social Welfare.

On March 11, 2019, a claim is promoted before the Transparency Regulator of the State of Quintana Roo because the Obligated Authority denies answering the petition 00117819.

Then, by Off. 089/2019 dated March 29, 2019, the obligated authority informs the following:

Órgano de Radicación judicial	Materia	Número de Juicios en Tramite por Periodo		
		Antes del 31 de diciembre de 1999	Del 01 de enero de 2000 al 31 de diciembre de 2010	Del 01 de enero de 2011 a la fecha
Junta Local de Conciliación y Arbitraje del Estado de Quintana Roo.	Laboral	48	620	1529
Junta Especial de Conciliación y Arbitraje Número 1 en Benito Juárez	Laboral	23	926	3218
Junta Especial de Conciliación y Arbitraje Número 2 en Benito Juárez	Laboral	39	2517	4004
Junta Especial de Conciliación y Arbitraje Número 3 en Benito Juárez	Laboral	0	1482	4290
Junta Especial de Conciliación y Arbitraje en Cozumel	Laboral	17	341	584
Junta Especial de Conciliación y Arbitraje en Solidaridad	Laboral	3	1807	4744
Tribunal de Conciliación y Arbitraje del Estado	Laboral	5	216	913

25. San Luis Potosi.

i. Bureaucratic Court of the State of San Luis Potosi.

Regarding the petition 00114919 in the grandfathered INFOMEX SLP software by Official Letter without number (WORD file), the obligated authority informs:

Petition 00114919

1.- 32 PROCEEDINGS SUBMITTED

2.- 5,015 PROCEEDINGS PRESENTED

3.- 8,214 PROCEEDINGS SUBMITTED

4.- THE DURATION OF THE JUDGMENTS THAT VENTURE WITHIN THIS STATE COURT OF CONCILIATION AND ARBITRATION IS DEPENDING ON THE ACTION EXERCISED BY THE ACTING PARTY (WORKER) AND THE MEANS OF DEFENSE THAT THE DEFENDANT PARTY OPPOSES (EXECUTIVE, LEGISLATIVE AND JUDICIAL BRANCHES, AS WELL AS THE 58 MUNICIPALITIES OF THE STATE), THE SAME OF THE EVIDENCE PROVIDED BY THE PARTIES AND THE PROCEDURAL IMPULSE THAT GIVES THEM THE SAME. "

ii.   Judicial Branch of the State of San Luis Potosi.

Regarding the petition 00114719, by Off. UT/145/2019 dated February 15, 2019, the Manager of the Transparency Unit of the Judicial Branch of the State of San Luis Potosi informs a disaggregated answer with the same proposition: *"These are data that are not reported, processed and recorded in the statistical system of this administrative body, so this Unit is not in a position to provide it."*.

iii.   Administrative Court of the State of San Luis Potosi.

Regarding the petition 00114819, by Official Letter without number dated February 14, 2019, the Chief of the Transparency Unit of the Administrative Court of the State of San Luis Potosi informs 255 pending cases, revealing the oldest one the case number 28/2006.

Moreover,   the   Obligated   Authority   says *"About your last request regarding the"* ADRLC*"(I request to know how long your* *trials take), I inform you that the average the duration is from 2 to 4 months, depending on the controversy."*

iv. Department of Labor and Social Welfare.

Regarding the petition 00115019 by the direct answer in the National Transparency Platform, the Responsible of the Information Unit of the Department of Labor and Social Welfare informs: *"... from 2004 to 2019 there are 8316 pending cases. The files are of labor matter. The Board of Conciliation and Arbitration has a bureau of entries. An EXCEL document is attached to the number of files. It is not possible to provide information regarding the quantum of claimed benefits since the information has not been captured. Now, about the average duration of a Trial, I inform you that it is not possible to provide an average since it is subject to the summary appeals or trials that the parties promote within the judgment of origin. "*

v. San Luis Potosi Attorney General.

On March 7, 2019, a claim is promoted before the Transparency Regulator of the State of San Luis Potosi because the Obligated Authority denies answering the petition 00200319; then, on the claim 337/2019, it informs:

AVERIGUACIONES PREVIAS	
TOTAL DE AVERIGUACIONES PREVIAS EN TRAMITE Y PENDIENTES DE RESOLVER	SD
TOTAL DE AVERIGUACIONES PREVIAS EN RESERVA**	5
CARPETAS DE INVESTIGACIÓN	
CARPETAS DE INVESTIGACIÓN EN TRAMITE Y PENDIENTES DE RESOLVER*	31259
CARPETAS DE INVESTIGACIÓN EN RESERVA	NA

SD. Son datos necesarios para poder generar la información solicitada

NA. No aplica, la figura de la reserva solo se aplica a las averiguaciones previas

* De los iniciados en 2018

** Resolutivo aplicados en el 2018

26. Sinaloa.

i. Board of Conciliation and Arbitration of the State of Sinaloa.

Regarding the petition 00114419, by Off. RDAEDyO-01.05 dated February 1, 2019, the Responsible of the Board of Conciliation and Arbitration of the State of Sinaloa informs the following labor law pending cases:

Board of Conciliation and Arbitration of the State of Sinaloa	
Period	Pending
Before Dec. 31, 1999	0
Jan. 1, 2000, to Dec. 31, 2010	664
Jan. 1, 2011- Act	5553
TOTAL	6217

ADRLC	18 Months

ii. Bureaucratic Court of the State of Sinaloa.

Regarding the petition 00183119, by direct answer uploaded in the grandfathered INFOMEX Sinaloa Software, the Obligated Authority informs the following pending bureaucratic labor law case in three PDF files attached:

Bureaucratic Labor Law cases pending			
Before Dec. 31, 1999	Jan. 1, 2000, to Dec. 31, 2010	Jan. 1, 2011,- Act	TOTAL
0	36	1347	1383

iii.   Administrative Court of the State of Sinaloa.

Regarding the petition 00190019, by Off. without number dated February 27, 2019, the Training Clerk of the Administrative Court of the State of Sinaloa informs 4,252 pending administrative law cases.

iv.   Supreme Court of Justice of the State of Sinaloa.

Regarding the petition 00114519, in an uploaded PDF file in the National Transparency Platform, the Obligated Authority disaggregates the pending legal cases between 2005 to 2018 in each of its Judicial Districts:

Pending Cases	
Period 2005-2018	
Civil, Commercial and Family Law	
Judicial District	**Number**
Ahome	10035
Angostura	265
Badiraguato	79
Concordia	202
Cosala	55
Culiacan	28058
Choix	145
Elota	637

Escuinapa	1819
El Fuerte	844
Guasave	2639
Mazatlan	12563
Mocorito	96
Rosario	2369
Salvador Alvarado	725
San Ignacio	464
Sinaloa	201
Navolato	3932
TOTAL	**65128**

v.   Sinaloa Attorney General.

Regarding the petition 00214719, by Off. without number dated February 28, 2019, the Responsible of the Transparency Unit of Sinaloa Attorney General informs the following pending criminal cases:

Sinaloa Attorney General			
System	Pending	Temporary File	TOTAL
TCJS	26039	153	26,192
NCJS	29,756	806	30,562

TOTAL	55,795	959	56,754

27. Sonora.

i. Sonora Attorney General.

Regarding the petition 00265419, by Off. DGTIC-0885/19 dated February 26, 2019, the General Manager of Technology and Communications of Sonora Attorney General informs the following pending criminal cases:

Sonora Attorney General.			
System	Pending	Temporary File	TOTAL
TCJS	331	26	357
NCJS	14,800	247	15047
TOTAL	15,131	264	15,404

ii. Administrative Court of the State of Sonora.

Regarding the petition *00165019*, by Off. 252/2019-P1 dated February 14, 2019, the General Clerk of the Administrative Court of the State of Sonora informs that there are no pending cases before December 31, 1999; that there are 944 pending cases (approximately) from the period January 1, 2000, to December 31, 2010; in addition to 6744 pending cases between January 1, 2011, to current day.

iii. Judicial Branch of the State of Sonora.

On February 8, 2019, an email is received from the Transparency Unit of the Judicial Branch of the State of Sonora, attaching it the Off. UT.-069/2019 dated the same day, where the petition 00165119 is attended, and the Obligated Authority informs that it will give data from the period 2008-2010 and 2011-2018 about Civil, Family, and Commercial Law cases. Furthermore, the authority will reveal TCJS data since 2000 and NCJS from December 15, 2015, until the current day.

Also, the Official Letter indicates that, by previous information and the litigation economic amount, there is no available information.

Finally, the Transparency Unit says that the pending cases apply the "*Device Principle*", where the advancement and conclusion go directly by the contestants, that said, if they do not move the case, the trial will be neither mover nor conclude.

In the attached EXCEL files to the answer, the following information is revealed:

2008-2010				
TOPIC	Presented	Resolution	Concluded	Pending
CIVIL	34449	10901	8857	14691
COMMERCIAL	71259	17509	31586	22164
FAMILY	63818	35588	4850	23380
TOTAL	169526	63998	45293	60,235

2011-2018				
TOPIC	Presented	Resolution	Concluded	Pending
CIVIL	82848	25324	15521	42003
COMMERCIAL	221729	43244	93774	84711
FAMILY	179380	79794	15205	84381
TOTAL	483957	148362	124500	211,095

Moreover, in the Attached EXCEL file (Criminal Law) there are 10,891 pending cases, noting the suspended cases and under prosecution of TCJS (6718 plus 1044) as well as 3219 pending NCJS cases.

Regarding the ADRLC, the obligated authority says: "The ADRLC *in the civil branch ranges from 10 to 14 months, according to the behavior of each year; The average duration of judgments concluded with judgment of the commercial cases ranges between 6 and 9 months, according to the behavior of each year; The average duration of judgments concluded with a ruling in the family law ranges between 4 and 6 months, depending on the behavior of each year; The average duration of criminal trials concluded with sentence in the traditional system from 2008 to 2016, ranges from 4 months to 6 months; For the year 2017, the average duration of traditional system trials is 1 to 2 months; The average duration of the trials that concluded in the oral trial stage with sentence, taking into consideration the date of entry to the control court until the sentence of oral trial ranges between 9 and 11 months. On the other hand, judgments concluded with a sentence by abbreviated procedure, have an average duration that ranges between two and five months. "*

iv. Department of Labor.

Regarding the petition 00165219, by Off. UT-011/2019 dated February 22, 2019, the Transparency Unit of the Department of Labor of the State of Sonora informs the content of the Off. PRJLCA-016/2019 with records since 1950:

BOARD OF CONCILIATION AND ARBITRATION OF THE STATE OF SONORA				
DISAGGREGATED	2011-2018	2000-2010	1950-1999	TOTAL
Undefined	23695	11078	854	35627
Active	1734	1396	3592	6722
Administrative File	108	33	4	145
Conciliated	350	126	0	476
Compliance with an agreement.	2697	2705	368	5770
Resolution compliance	72	471	439	982
Dismissed	6778	13108	6047	25933
Non Jurisdiction	30	105	193	328
Rest plaintiffs	0	0	97	97
Concluded	2081	4653	4363	11097
TOTAL	37545	33675	15957	87177
Source. President of the Board of Conciliation and Arbitration of the State of Sonora.				

Moreover, in the Off. PRJLCA-016/2019, the President of the Board of informs that the ADRLC is two years.

28. Tabasco.

i.   Supreme Court of Justice of the State of Tabasco.

On February 22, 2019, a claim is promoted against the Obligated Authority because the National Transparency Platform has an error where the answer cannot be downloaded. Moreover, in the grandfathered INFOMEX Tabasco platform, the Off. TSJ/UT/175/19 contains a different petition warning.

ii. Administrative Court of the State of Tabasco.

On February 20, 2019, a claim is promoted against the Obligated Authority because there is an error to download the answer through the National Transparency Platform. Independently to that situation, in the grandfathered INFOMEX Tabasco software, by Resolution Agreement dated February 12, 2019, the authority answers the petition 00354819.

Finally, the Obligated Authority informs that the ADRLC is 228 days approximately between the presentation date of the legal case and the resolution date of the appeal.

iii. General Coordinator of Legal Cases.

Regarding the petition 00354919, by Availability Agreement dated February 7, 2019, the Chief of the Transparency Department of the General Coordinator of Legal Cases informs 4 bureaucratic labor law cases pending cases that started before December 31, 1999; 84 from the period January 1, 2000 to December 31, 2010 and 146 from January 1, 2011 to current day, with a litigation economic amount charged to the State Budget of $7,706,811.77.

iv. State Employment Office.

Regarding the petition 00355019, by Off., CS/UT/004/2019 dated February 19, 2019; the Transparency Unit of the Obligated Authority informs 17 pending labor law cases.

    v. Department of Government.

Regarding the petition 00355119, the obligated authority informs the following:

SEGOB JLCA

- en cuanto hace el periodo comprendido del mes de enero a diciembre del ejercicio mil novecientos noventa y ocho se registró ante esta Autoridad laboral un total de ciento diecinueve demandas laborales, mismos que continúan con su etapa procesal correspondiente.

- en cuanto hace el periodo comprendido del mes de enero a diciembre del ejercicio mil novecientos noventa y nueve se registró ante esta Autoridad laboral un total de ciento sesenta y dos demandas laborales, mismos que continúan con su etapa procesal correspondiente.

  (ANEXO 1. el cual contiene órgano de radicación Judicial, materia, número de expediente y estatus, con la finalidad de mayor apreciación y certeza jurídica)

Por otra parte, para dar cumplimiento a lo peticionado en el segundo cuestionamiento realizado tal como se menciona en líneas que anteceden esta Autoridad Laboral contesta lo siguiente:

- Se hace del conocimiento del solicitante que este Tribunal Laboral se encuentra imposibilitado para rendir el informe solicitado por lo que hace a las prestaciones reclamadas de cada juicio laboral, en virtud que el Reglamento Interno de la Junta Local de Conciliación y Arbitraje no obliga que se lleve un registro a nivel detalle.

- en cuanto hace el periodo comprendido del mes de enero a diciembre del ejercicio dos mil se registró ante esta Autoridad laboral un total de doscientos uno demandas laborales, mismos que continúan con su etapa procesal correspondiente.

- en cuanto hace el periodo comprendido del mes de enero a diciembre del ejercicio dos mil uno se registró ante esta Autoridad laboral un total de ciento noventa y ocho demandas laborales, mismos que continúan con su etapa procesal correspondiente.

- en cuanto hace el periodo comprendido del mes de enero a diciembre del ejercicio dos mil dos se registró ante esta Autoridad laboral un total de doscientos dos demandas laborales, mismos que continúan con su etapa procesal correspondiente.

- en cuanto hace el periodo comprendido del mes de enero a diciembre del ejercicio dos mil tres se registró ante esta Autoridad laboral un total de treinta y cuatro demandas laborales, mismos que continúan con su etapa procesal correspondiente.

- en cuanto hace el periodo comprendido del mes de enero a diciembre del ejercicio dos mil cuatro se registró ante esta Autoridad laboral un total de cuatrocientos setenta y dos demandas laborales, mismos que continúan con su etapa procesal correspondiente.

- en cuanto hace el periodo comprendido del mes de enero a diciembre del ejercicio dos mil cinco se registró ante esta Autoridad laboral un total de cuatrocientos diez demandas laborales, mismos que continúan con su etapa procesal correspondiente.

- en cuanto hace el periodo comprendido del mes de enero a diciembre del ejercicio dos mil seis se registró ante esta Autoridad laboral un total de cuatrocientos cincuenta y cinco demandas laborales, mismos que continúan con su etapa procesal correspondiente.

- en cuanto hace el periodo comprendido del mes de enero a diciembre del ejercicio dos mil siete se registró ante esta Autoridad laboral un total de ciento noventa demandas laborales de los cuales se concluyeron tres juicios laborales.

- en cuanto hace el periodo comprendido del mes de enero a diciembre del ejercicio dos mil ocho se registró ante esta Autoridad laboral un total de cuatrocientos trece demandas laborales de los cuales se concluyeron veinte juicios laborales.

SEGOB   JLCA

- en cuanto hace el periodo comprendido del mes de enero a diciembre del ejercicio dos mil nueve se registró ante esta Autoridad laboral un total de cuatrocientos setenta y ocho demandas laborales de los cuales se concluyeron dieciséis juicios laborales

- en cuanto hace el periodo comprendido del mes de enero a diciembre del ejercicio dos mil diez se registró ante esta Autoridad laboral un total de quinientos noventa demandas laborales de los cuales se concluyeron veintisiete juicios laborales.

  (ANEXO 2 el cual contiene órgano de radicación Judicial, materia, número de expediente y estatus, con la finalidad de mayor apreciación y certeza jurídica)

Por otra parte, para dar cumplimiento a lo peticionado en el tercer cuestionamiento realizado tal como se menciona en líneas que anteceden esta Autoridad Laboral contesta lo siguiente:

- Se hace del conocimiento del solicitante que este Tribunal Laboral se encuentra imposibilitado para rendir el informe solicitado por lo que hace a las prestaciones reclamadas de cada juicio laboral, en virtud que el Reglamento Interno de la Junta Local de Conciliación y Arbitraje no obliga que se lleve un registro a nivel detalle; por

- en cuanto hace el periodo comprendido del mes de enero a diciembre del ejercicio dos mil once se registró ante esta Autoridad laboral un total de diecinueve demandas laborales de los cuales se concluyeron dos juicios laborales.

- en cuanto hace el periodo comprendido del mes de enero a diciembre del ejercicio dos mil doce se registró ante esta Autoridad laboral un total de setecientas setecientos tres demandas laborales de los cuales se concluyeron ciento trece juicios laborales.

- en cuanto hace el periodo comprendido del mes de enero a diciembre del ejercicio dos mil trece se registró ante esta Autoridad laboral un total de quinientos setenta y tres demandas laborales de los cuales se concluyeron noventa y tres juicios laborales.

- en cuanto hace el periodo comprendido del mes de enero a diciembre del ejercicio dos mil catorce se registró ante esta Autoridad laboral un total de quinientos diez demandas laborales de los cuales se concluyeron doscientos veintitrés juicios laborales.

- en cuanto hace el periodo comprendido del mes de enero a diciembre del ejercicio dos mil quince se registró ante esta Autoridad laboral un total de cuatrocientos cuarenta y ocho demandas laborales de los cuales se concluyeron quinientos noventa y ocho demandas laborales.

- en cuanto hace el periodo comprendido del mes de enero a diciembre del ejercicio dos mil dieciséis se registró ante esta Autoridad laboral un total de trescientos ochenta y tres demandas laborales de los cuales se concluyeron unas mil cuatrocientas noventa y nueve demandas laborales.

- en cuanto hace el periodo comprendido del mes de enero a diciembre del ejercicio dos mil diecisiete se registró ante esta Autoridad laboral un total de doscientos setenta y siete demandas laborales de los cuales se concluyeron novecientos noventa y ocho demandas laborales.

- en cuanto hace el periodo comprendido del mes de enero a diciembre del ejercicio dos mil dieciocho se registró ante esta Autoridad laboral un total de ciento veinte demandas laborales de los cuales se concluyeron cuatrocientos diez demandas laborales.

- en cuanto hace el periodo comprendido del mes de enero a febrero del ejercicio dos mil diecinueve se registraron ante esta Autoridad laboral un total de una demanda laboral.

(ANEXO 3 el cual contiene órgano de radicación Judicial, materia, número de expediente y estatus, con la finalidad de mayor apreciación y certeza jurídica)

Por otra parte, para dar cumplimiento a lo peticionado en el cuarto cuestionamiento realizado tal como se menciona en líneas que anteceden hago de conocimiento al solicitante que en este Tribunal se desahogan diferentes etapas procesales tal y como lo establece en los numerales 871 al 890 de la Ley Federal del Trabajo, no se tiene una fecha específica para dar por terminado el expediente laboral, en virtud que cada juicio laboral son diferentes controversias laborales.

vi. Tabasco Attorney General.

Regarding the petition 00465619 by Off. 2624/2019 dated March 13, 2019, the obligated authority informs:

En respuesta al oficio FGE/UTAIP/0151/2019, en donde solicita información de carpetas de investigación del nuevo sistema de justicia penal que se encuentra en archivo temporal, le comunico que en el año 2018 se mandaron al archivo temporal 15,360 carpetas de investigación, y en cuanto a las averiguaciones previas, en el año 2018 es cero.

29. Tamaulipas

i. Administrative Court of the State of Tamaulipas.

Regarding the petition 00072319, by Off. TJA/UT/033/2019 dated February 19, 2019; the Chief of the Transparency Department of the Administrative Court of the State of Tamaulipas informs the content of the Official Letters given by the Three Justices of each of the Unitary Courts, consisting of 144 pending administrative legal cases with a litigation economic amount charged to the State Budget of $23,043,325.19.

ii. Administrative Court of Victoria.

By Official Letter, TJAM/UT/002/2019 dated March 1, 2019, the Chief of the Transparency Unit of the Administrative Court of Victoria answers the petition 00072419 saying that 54 legal cases are pending, with a litigation economic amount of $136,053.00 charged to the City Town Budget.

iii. Judicial Branch of the State of Tamaulipas.

Regarding the petition 00072519, by Off. CPDA y E/053/2019 dated February 25, 2019; the Responsible of the Statistics and Transparency Bureau of the Judicial Branch of the State of Tamaulipas informs the following pending cases:

Judicial Branch of the State of Tamaulipas.			
Before Dec. 31, 1999	Jan. 1, 2000, to Dec. 31, 2010	Jan. 1, 2011- Act	TOTAL
30	349	33,566	33,945

It is essential to say that the disaggregated information reveals the oldest pending case, case number 00814/1975 of the First Family Court of Matamoros.

iv. Department of Labor.

Regarding the petition 0072619, by Off. DJYAIP/018/2019, Off. DJYAIP/017/2019 and Off. DJYAIP/025/2019 attached in an EXCEL DATABASE, the Obligated Authority informs the following labor law pending cases:

Labor Law pending cases (Tamaulipas)			
Before Dec. 31, 1999	Jan. 1, 2000, to	Jan. 1, 2011,- Act	TOTAL

	Dec. 31, 2010		
20	487	1366	1873

Also, the Obligated Authority reveals the existence of a labor law pending case, case number 00058/E03/1977, of the Special Board Number Three, that said, 40 years of a labor dispute.

v. Tamaulipas Attorney General.

Regarding the petition 00158819, the obligated authority informs as follows (Off. 5920/2019):

En virtud de lo solicitado, y de conformidad con el artículo 146 numeral 1 de la Ley de Transparencia y Acceso a la Información Pública de Tamaulipas, se hace de su conocimiento que se giró oficio a las áreas responsables de la información requerida quienes notificaron a esta Unidad de Transparencia lo descrito a continuación.

Solicito saber cuántas averiguaciones previas del sistema tradicional de justicia penal se encuentran en trámite y pendientes de resolver
Respuesta: 148,929

Solicito saber cuántas averiguaciones previas del sistema tradicional de justicia penal se encuentran en la reserva.
Respuesta: 16,082

Solicito saber cuántas carpetas de investigación del nuevo sistema de justicia penal se encuentran en trámite y pendientes de resolver, así como aquellas que se encuentren en la reserva
Respuesta: 76,112 en trámite.

30. Tlaxcala.

i. Supreme Court of Justice of the State of Tlaxcala and Judiciary Council.

Regarding the petition 00051419, by Agreement dated February 18, 2019; the Intern Chief of the Transparency Unit of the Obligated Authority informs the Off. 191/C/2019 signed by the Comptroller of the Supreme Court of Justice of the State of Tlaxcala, reporting that there is no available information, attaching an Official Paper dated February 12, 2019.

Independently to that situation, the Obligated Authority informs that the ADRLC, pondering the average of days from the beginning until the resolution of the case, in 400 days for Criminal Law cases, 260 days for Civil Law cases; 140 days for Commercial disputes and 150 for Family Law inquiries.

ii. Bureaucratic Labor Court of the State of Tlaxcala.

Regarding the petition 00051519, by Off. without number dated March 8, 2019; the Chief of the Transparency Unit of the Obligated Authority informs the following pending cases (contained in an EXCEL Database):

Bureaucratic Labor Law pending cases (Tlaxcala)			
Before Dec. 31, 1999	Jan. 1, 2000, to Dec. 31, 2010	Jan. 1, 2011,- Act	TOTAL
7	493	1192	1692

According to the available information of 398 pending cases (at least), there is a litigation economic amount charged to the State Budget of $191, 318,489.50.

Regarding the ADRLC, the Obligated Authority says: "...THAT CAN NOT BE DETERMINED, IN SO FAR THAT THEY ARE SUBJECT TO THE PROCEDURAL IMPULSE OF THE PARTIES, THIS IS, PROMOTIONS, DISCHARGE OF EVIDENCE, POSSESSION OF INCIDENTS, AND / OR OTHER MEANS OF RESOURCE THAT CONTEMPLATES THE LAW IN THE MATTERS, APPEAL OF SUCH RESOLUTIONS AND THE TIME IN WHICH THE COURTS OF THE FEDERAL FIRE RESOLVE THEM AMONG OTHER THINGS. "

iii. Department of Government.

Regarding the petitions 00102719 and 00072919, by Off. SGT/221/2019 dated March 7, 2019; the Chief of the Transparency Unit of the Department of Government informs the content of the Official Letter number C.I.UT-20-19 dated March 5, 2019; where the Responsible of Legal Support of the Board of Conciliation and Arbitration of the State of Tlaxcala reveals 3560 pending labor law cases, being the oldest on the case C.D.T. 3/1961-3TII, a labor law case of 55 years of disputation.

Moreover, in the Off. C.I. UT-19-19 dated February 18, 2019; the disaggregated information is presented as follows:

"How many labor lawsuits that began before December 31, 1999, are pending and unfinished.

17 Active processes.

Attached is list 1.1 with the file numbers, subject, and judicial filing body.

How many labor lawsuits that began between January 1, 2000, and December 31, 2010, are in process and not concluded.

578 active processes.

Attached is list 1.2 with the file numbers, subject matter, and judicial filing body.

How many labor lawsuits that began between January 1, 2011, and the current date are in and pending and not concluded.

2965 Active processes.

Attached is list 1.3 with the file numbers, subject matter, and judicial filing body.

Note: in each of the above tables it is indicated which files are in the execution period of the award, same in which the trial has concluded with the issuance of a prize, but the labor dispute has not finished.

On the other hand, it is noted that compact disc containing electronic files called "Application lists 00072919" in Excel, and PDF format containing the lists 1.1, 1.2 and 1.3 mentioned in the previous points are added to this trade.

The average duration of labor trials and judgments depends on different factors, including the willingness of the parties to reach an agreement, the defense strategy of the parties, incidents, resources, and amparos promoted, as well as the evidence offered. The duration of the same can be brief or very prolonged.

Below is the average data that takes labor processes:

	ADRLC
The average duration of cases resolved (terminated) by Agreement, Withdrawal, Completed Award, Absolutory Award, Limitation, and Expiration.	*1.5 years.*
Average time in which a resolution that puts an end to judgment (decision) is issued.	*4.49 years*

iv. Tlaxcala Attorney General.

Regarding the petition 00113419, by Off. 300/2019 dated april 8, 2019, the obligated authority informs the following:

PERIOD	CURRENT NCJS CASES	RESERVE NCJS CASES	CONCLUDED NCJS CASES
JUNE 18 2016-DECEMBER 31 2016	2917	401	394
2017	4369	1005	1217
2018	9835	869	2635

31. Veracruz.

    i. Judicial Branch.

Regarding the petition 00189819, by Off. UTAIPPJE/0306/2019 dated March 19, 2019; the Chief of the Transparency Unit of the Judicial Branch of the State of Veracruz *"...authorizes unanimously the measures designed to allow the consultation of the documents through the direct consultation modality."*

    ii. Administrative Court of the State of Veracruz.

Regarding the petition 00189919, by Off. TEJAV/UT/38/2019 dated February 18, 2019; the Chief of the Transparency Unit of the Administrative Court of the State of Veracruz reveals the following pending cases:

ADMINISTRATIVE LAW PENDING CASES		
ADMINISTRATIVE COURT OF THE STATE OF VERACRUZ		
Court	Pending to January 31, 2019	Oldest Case.
First Unitary Court	330	57/2009
Second Unitary Court	626	023/2005
Third Unitary Court	584	47/2009/3a-II
Fourth Unitary Court	586	01/2013-III
TOTAL	2126	-

Moreover, according to the litigation economic amount disaggregated in the Third Unitary Court (pending cases), the disputes represent $345, 435,783.79 (at least).

iii. Department of Labor, Social Welfare and Productivity.

Regarding the petition 00190019, by Off. STPSP/UT/177/2019 dated February 27, 2019; the Chief of the Transparency Unit of the Obligated Authority reveals 10,021 pending labor law cases at least.

Moreover, the authority says *"... it has been given the knowledge that it is not possible to determine the duration of the resolution of labor cases due to the complexity of each of these."*

iv. Veracruz Attorney General.

Regarding the petition 00404619, by Off. 489/2019 dated March 8, 2019; the Deputy Director of Personal Data informs the following 2018 pending criminal law cases:

Veracruz Attorney General			
System	Process	Reserve	TOTAL
TCJS	75	662	737
NCJS	43,483	12195	55,678
TOTAL	43,558	12,857	56,415

32. Yucatan.

i. Governor's Office; Department of Economic Promotion and Labor and General Department of Government.

Regarding the petition *00111219*, by Resolution dated February 1, 2019, signed by the Legal Manager and Chief of the Transparency Unit of the Department of Economic Promotion and Labor, it is informed the NON-JURISDICTION of the obligated authority, suggesting to ask the General Department of Government.

On the other side, by petition 00116219 uploaded directly in the National Transparency Platform, the General Department of Government says: "... this information cannot be provided since it is not a matter of access to public information, which is not the faculty of this obliged subject.". *The obligated authority attaches a WORD file that is broken down.*

Finally, in the petition 00111019, the Governor's Office answers in the National Transparency Platform with non-existent information, without attaching any answer.

Considering the content of the answers given by the obligated authority, by permission to deny public information of labor law cases, three claims are promoted before the Transparency Regulator of the State of Yucatan.

The arguments are that none of the authorities (including the Governor of Yucatan) reveals the information of labor law pending cases in the asked periods (pending cases before December 31, 1999; between January 1, 2000, to December 31, 2010, and from January 1, 2011, to current day) and the ADRLC.

Also, there is no catalog where the authority Board of Conciliation and Arbitration of the State of Yucatan appears available because the institutional reform by Decree 5/2018 published in the Official Journal of Yucatan on November 23, 2018.

Then, on the claim 141/2019, the obligated authority reveals **8846 pending labor law cases (at least).**

ii. Legal Counsel of the State of Yucatan.

Regarding the petition 00111119 by the direct answer in the grandfathered INFOMEX Yucatan software, the Obligated Authority informs ten pending bureaucratic labor law cases with a litigation amount charged to the State Budget of $2, 881, 730.75.

iii. Supreme Court of Justice of the State of Yucatan.

Regarding the petition *00110619* by Resolution dated February 5, 2019; the Chief of the Transparency Unit of the Supreme Court of Justice of the State of

Yucatan declares the notorious non-jurisdiction of the Obligated Authority, suggesting to ask the Judiciary Council of the State of Yucatan.

iv. Judiciary Council of the State of Yucatan.

Regarding the petition 00110919, by Resolution dated March 6, 2019; the Responsible of the Transparency Unit of the Judiciary Council of the State of Yucatan informs 15,485 pending civil and commercial law cases, (Available information since May 11, 2009). Now, it is essential to say that the litigation economic amount of those cases is $2, 459, 613,706.96 (at least).

Moreover, the Obligated Authority informs the following data:

TOPIC	ADRLC (days)
Civil Law	279
Commercial Law	254
General Average	264

v. Administrative Court of the State of Yucatan.

Regarding the petition 00110519, by Official Letter without number signed by the Responsible of the Transparency Unit of the Obligated Authority, it is informed the history of the institutional changes the Administrative Court had experienced.

Moreover, the authority says "... *The trials that were published before December 31, 1999, to February 28, 2011, filed before the Contentious-Administrative Tribunal, the same account that has information from January 1, 2007, to January 31, 2010, which is of 100 files that are in process. ... However, the trials that were published before December 31, 1999, to February 28, 2011, were presented before the Contentious-Administrative Tribunal. The trials that began on March 1, 2011, to June 20, 2014, were presented before the Electoral and*

Administrative Justice Court of the Judicial Branch of the State of Yucatan. The trials that began on June 21, 2014, to July 18, 2017, were presented before the Fiscal and Administrative Justice Court of the Judicial Branch of the State of Yucatan. In this period of validity from January 1, 2011, to the date of your request: it is 648 records that are in the world ... We inform you that the processes are in the light of administrative law and the Organic Act of the Court of Administrative Justice, both of this State, and of the procedural operation of the parties, the complexity of the matter, the resolution of the problem, as well as the relief or improvement of the evidence. However, according to the experience of this court, it could be estimated in approximately one year."

vi. Administrative Court of Merida.

Regarding the petition 00110819, by Off. **No. TCAMM.31.2019,** dated February 18, 2019, the Chief of the Transparency Unit of the Administrative Court of Merida informs:

"The determination of the inexistence of the requested information is confirmed with a date before January 16, 2016, because the Court began its functions after that date.

The reservation classification is confirmed to the information regarding the file number, and quantum of benefits claimed from the files that are being processed in the Court, based on the grounds and reasons indicated in the Agreement.

The applicant is informed that the number of open files that are being processed by the Court, with a date after January 16, 2016, is 95 records. The matter of the data is the Administrative and Municipal Tax Litigation. The filing body is the Administrative Court of Merida.

Finally, the applicant is informed that the information requested after January 16, 2016, which is found in files that have caused a state, can be consulted on the Court's website at the link http: //tcam.gob. mx / within the "Resolutions" section, where the public versions of the judgments of the completed files are available, which contain the information regarding the file number and quantum of claimed benefits, as well as the data necessary to determine the average duration of the resolutions issued by this Court. "

vii. Bureaucratic Labor Court of the State of Yucatan.

Regarding the petition *00110719*, by Resolution dated February 13, 2019, the Chief of the Transparency Unit of the Obligated Authority informs the existence of an EXCEL Data Base with the pending cases before the Bureaucratic Court (4442 records). In the Data Base, there are three registers from 1988, cases 7/88 and 14/88, related to DPV (Progreso Bureau of Roads and Protection) and the case 28/88 of Timizin.

Moreover, the authority says that the ADRLC is two years, but the process inactivity might delay the Bureaucratic Labor trial.

viii. Yucatan Attorney General.

Regarding the petition 00225119, by Off. 461/2019 dated March 4, 2019; the Manager of the Department of Investigation and Early Attention of Yucatan Attorney General informs:

TOPIC	ANSWER
TCJS pending cases.	173, 559
TCJS reserve cases.	1,520
NCJS pending cases.	8,519
NCJS reserve cases	12,127

33. Zacatecas.

i. Zacatecas Attorney General.

Regarding the petition 00149119, by answer content in a PDF file (uploaded in the National Transparency Platform), the Transparency Unit of Zacatecas Attorney General informs the following pending cases:

Zacatecas Attorney General			
System	Process	Temporary File	TOTAL
TCJS	249	1140	1689
NCJS	10,062	5,231	15,293
TOTAL	10,311	6,671	16,982

ii.   Supreme Court of Justice of the State of Zacatecas.

Regarding the petition 00090419, by Off. UT-107/2019 dated February 22, 2019; the Chief of the Transparency Unit informs:

"... being that the information is not processed or systematized to be provided in the terms required by the applicant, in accordance with articles 96 and 98 of the Transparency and Access to Public Information of the State of Zacatecas Act for the case that it is useful, the mentioned statistics can be consulted in the Quarterly Bulletins that are published permanently for consultation and reproduction in the electronic portal: http://www.tsjzac.gob.mx/, main page, Transparency section, section "Article 39. Obligations of Common Transparency of all obligated subjects", "Fraction XXX. Statistics generated. "

However, following the principle of maximum publicity, and if it is useful, the applicant is informed that in the statistical annexes that make up the annual report provided by the Presidency of this Court may consult the historical data of the pending matters of each jurisdictional body. Due to the length of each document, it is available at the following electronic links:

...

...

With the preceding, access to public information has been granted according to the formats and information generated in compliance with the faculties, powers or functions conferred on the Superior Court of Justice of the State of Zacatecas, as they are found in the archives, and for its knowledge, it is notified through the National Transparency Platform and the email account provided in accordance with the provisions of articles 94 and 102 of the Transparency and Access to Public Information of the State of Zacatecas Act. "

Now, the revealed information in electronic websites contains the Annual Report of the Supreme Court of Justice of the State of Zacatecas, with the following data:

SUPREME COURT OF JUSTICE OF THE STATE OF ZACATECAS				
Year	Pending cases from previous years	Received	Concluded	Pending
2000	25802	22882	19178	29506
2001	24939	20570	18542	26867
2002	26867	27906	24917	29856
2003	N/A			
2004	21039	25272	23305	25782
2005	55350		27732	27618
2006	56388		26265	30123
2007	30123	25059	20467	34715
2008	34715	25378	19811	

2009	40282	23690	14865	49107
2010	70958		21736	49222
2011	49222	27312	19276	57258
2012	57258	23316	22552	58022
2013	58022	22027	22968	57081
2014	57081	21661	18662	60080
2015	60080	21176	17563	63693
2016	63693	20607	17040	67260
2017	67260	25295	N/A	N/A
2018	N/A	27711	N/A	N/A
PENDING CASES (ESTIMATE) **				70,000
**Calculated by the disaggregation and judicial statistics of the obligated authority.				
Source: Annual Report 2000-2018				

iii. Administrative Court of the State of Zacatecas.

Regarding the petition 00090519, by Off. 14/2019 dated February 26, 2019, the Chief of the Transparency Unit of the Administrative Court of the State of Zacatecas informs 242 pending cases.

Moreover, the authority says "... *The time it takes to resolve a trial depends on the dispositive principle, which consists of the power that the parties have to carry and promote a process, having the right to begin and/or answer in a trial, as well as to participate in it and perform the actions that are appropriate to their rights. It should also be mentioned that this H. Tribunal strictly adheres to the provisions and terms established in the Administrative Justice Act to guarantee an effective right of access to Justice.*"

iv. Public Defender Institute.

Regarding the petition 00090919, by Off. without number dated February 26, 2019, the Chief of the Transparency Unit of the Obligated Authority informs 1,165 pending cases that represent by the Office of the Defense of Labor before the Board of Conciliation and Arbitration of the State of Zacatecas, as well as 193 pending bureaucratic law cases before the Bureaucratic Labor Court of the State of Zacatecas.

v. General Department of Government.

Regarding the petition 00091019, by Off. SGG/UT/268/2019 dated March 1, 2019, the Chief of the Transparency Unit of the Obligated Authority reveals 1954 pending bureaucratic labor law cases before the Bureaucratic Labor Court and 6,870 pending labor law cases before the Board of Conciliation and Arbitration; disaggregated data attach the information.

In addition to the full information, the authority says that ADRLC before the Bureaucratic Labor Court is two years and one year (approximately) before the Board of Conciliation and Arbitration.

vi. General Counsel.

Regarding the petition 00091119, by Off. C.G.J./D.A.C./0177/2019 dated February 19, 2019, the Manager of Litigation of the General Council of Zacatecas Government informs 20 pending labor law cases with a litigation economic amount charged to the State Budget of $886,413.02 (at least).

Part. C. Petitions and claims (Summary).

- Closing this book edition, 220 Obligated Authorities were asked to reveal public information and Judicial Statistics.

- There were 204 answers, pending 3 (98.55%).

- In 198 answers, 44 claims were promoted (22.22%) because of lack of transparency.

- From 44 claims, 34 were solved and 10 pending, as follows:.

TABLERO DE CONTROL CONTENCIOSO (SPANISH RECORDS)				
RECURSOS DE REVISIÓN ANTE ORGANISMOS GARANTES				
Organismo Garante	Expediente	Sujeto Obligado	STATUS	SENTIDO RESOLUCIÓN
INAI	RRA 1005/19	Tribunal Superior Agrario	Resuelto	Confirma
INAI	RRA 1013/19	Tribunal Superior Agrario	Resuelto	Sobresee
DURANGO	RR/58/19	Tribunal de Justicia Administrativa Durango	Resuelto	Confirma
JALISCO	RR 238/2019	Supremo Tribunal Justicia Jalisco	Substanciación	Sobresee
MORELOS	572/2019	Consejo de la Judicatura	Pendiente de resolver	
MORELOS	573/2019	Tribunal Superior de Justicia	Pendiente de resolver	
OAXACA	RRAI 43/2019	Junta de Conciliación Agraria	Resuelto	Información disponible
INAI	RRA 1461/19	PROFEDET	Resuelto	Información disponible
INAI	RRA 1463/19	SEGOB	Resuelto	Sobresee y confirma
GUANAJUATO	-	Poder Judicial del Estado de GTO.	Sin notificar admisión	
INAI	RRA 1530/19	Consejo de la Judicatura Federal	Resuelto	Confirma
YUCATÁN	RR 142/2019	Fomento Económico y Trabajo	Resuelto	Confirma

YUCATÁN	RR 140/2019	Despacho Gobernador	Resuelto	Modifica
YUCATÁN	RR 141/2019	SEGOB YUCATÁN	Resuelto	Revoca, información disponible
YUCATÁN	RR 155/2019	Consejería Jurídica Edo.	Desistido	Información disponible
BAJA CALIFORNIA	REV 62/2019	TJA BAJA CALIFORNIA	Resuelto	Revoca, información disponible
COLIMA	RR PNT 150/2019	PODER EJECUTIVO	Resuelto	Revoca, información disponible
TABASCO	-	Coordinación Gral. Asuntos Jurídicos.	Sin notificar admisión	
TABASCO	-	TJA Tabasco	Sin notificar admisión	
TLAXCALA	RR 59/2019	Consejería Jurídica	Desistido	Información disponible
TLAXCALA	RR 61/2019	SEGOB TLAXCALA	Desistido	Información disponible
BAJA CALIFORNIA SUR	RRI 40/2019	H. Tribunal Superior Justicia BCJ	Substanciació n	
INAI	RRA 1884/19	Fiscalía General de la República	Resuelto	Modifica
INAI	RRA 1903/19	S.R.E.	Resuelto	Información disponible
CHIHUAHUA	149/2019	STPS	Resuelto	Información disponible
DURANGO	RR/59/19	STPS	Resuelto	Información Disponible
NUEVO LEÓN	RR 38/2019	TRIBUNAL CONCILIACIÓN ARBITRAJE NL	Resuelto	Información disponible
NUEVO LEÓN	RR 39/2019	T. Contencioso Administrativo. NL.	Resuelto	Información disponible
TABASCO	-	Tribunal Superior de Justicia de Tabasco	Sin notificar admisión	
MORELOS	604/2019	Fiscalía General de Morelos	Resuelto	Sobresee y sin materia.
OAXACA	R.R.A.I 74/2019	JLCA OAXACA	Resuelto	Fundado
INAI	RRA 2178/19	STPS	Resuelto	Información disponible

COLIMA	RR PNT 160/2019	Fiscalía General de Colima	Resuelto	Información disponible
BAJA CALIFORNIA SUR	RRI 64/2019	STPS-JLCA	Substanciación	
GUERRERO	-	Fiscalía General Guerrero	Resuelto	Desecha
BAJA CALIFORNIA	62/2019	TJA BAJA CALIFORNIA	Resuelto	Información disponible
COLIMA	RR PNT/171/2019	PODER EJECUTIVO	Resuelto	Información disponible
QUINTANA ROO	PNTRR/186/2019	STPS	Resuelto	Sobresee
JALISCO	-	Fiscalía Estatal de Jalisco	Resuelto	Información disponible
INAI	RRA 2704/19	CJEF	Resuelto	Información disponible
COAHUIILA	288/2019	Fiscalía Estatal de Coahuila	Resuelto	Información disponible
NAYARIT	-	STPS	Sin notificar admisión	
NAYARIT	-	STPS	Sin notificar admisión	
DURANGO	RR/99/19	Fiscalía General del Estado de Durango	Resuelto	Información disponible

IV.   Comments to Constitutional Controversy case INEGI v. INAI.

Before the Supreme Court of Justice of the Nation, the Constitutional Controversy case *INEGI v. INAI*[54] is argued because of a supposed jurisdiction interference grieved by claim resolutions of INAI obligating to INEGI to reveal information.

Previously, it was mentioned that the author is the petitioner of the claim that caused the Constitutional Controversy case 214/2018, where SCJN decided a Caution to avoid the claim RRA 6844/18 accomplishment.

Background as a case, on February 7, 2014, it was published on the Federal Official Journal the Constitutional Reform of Transparency and Access to Public Information. Then, in 2015 and 2016, regulations are issued.

The essential purpose of the Constitutional Reform was to amplify the fundamental right of Access to information through institutional transparency, public accountability, and personal data protection guarantees. Also, the reform focused on every person must reveal the Public Resource received and executed.

During the legislative process, one of the essential purposes is to create a National Transparency and Public Information System by INAI, Superior Auditor of the Federation, the General Archive of the Nation, INEGI and the Transparency Regulators of the 32 states of Mexico, to coordinate a "*... better articulation of the policies and actions that each organization carries out in its respective spheres of competence and thereby contribute to a better Public Accountability in Mexico*". (Mexico's Senate Dictum, December 19, 2012, page 41)[55].

During the legislative discussion, it is essential to mention the words of the Senators saying "*... What we are going to vote today is a reform of the transparency regime, which seeks to exercise the right of access to public information of the governed. The full exercise of this right is the purpose of this reform, and therefore*

---

[54] Cases number 117/2018, 214/2018, and 9/2019.

[55] Available in http://legislacion.scjn.gob.mx/Buscador/Paginas/wfProcesoLegislativoCompleto.aspx?q=b/EcoMjef uFeB6DOaNOimNPZPsNLFqe0s7fey1FqrifPEDNz/vsxqtYAffSzMf0n+QavH/2FZJBQGSnpUtAVFQ ==

this reform involves changes that lay the foundations ... (Continues 22nd part) ... involves changes that lay the foundation for the establishment of a National System of Transparency and Access to Public Information, through a legal and procedural framework that provides greater facilities and greater guarantees for the people, being the central subject of the reform" (Mexico's Senate discussion, November 20, 2013)[56].

Well, the Transparency, Access to Public Information and Personal Data Protection regulations rule the National System with essential functions related to the fundamental right of Access to public information.

Following these directives, on March 5, 2018, on the Federal Official Journal is published the National Transparency and Access to Information Program 2017-2021, where that fundamental right has a thematic strategy between the whole authorities of the National System, including INAI and INEGI. Under these circumstances, the fundamental right of Access to information is the core goal of institutions and regulators.

The Constituent Reformer intention in transparency and essential content of the fundamental right to Access to public information answers a liberal constitutional logic: Mexico has institutions that integrate a National System that must reveal the public accountability of the Federal Funds.

Under this perspective, there is no jurisdiction interference controversy because of the institutional responsibility to guarantee the essential content of the fundamental right of Access to public information, according to the Constituent Reformer to create a National Transparency and Public Information System.

Therefore, INEGI, in the National System, cannot grieve of INAI resolutions, because both institutions have a Constitutional duty to reveal all the information they produce. Article 6, section A, clause I, from the Political Constitution of the United States of Mexico, establishes an institutional guarantee of the fundamental right of access to public information:

---

[56] Available in http://legislacion.scjn.gob.mx/Buscador/Paginas/wfProcesoLegislativoCompleto.aspx?q=b/EcoMjef uFeB6DOaNOimNPZPsNLFqe0s7fey1FqrifPEDNz/vsxqtYAffSzMf0nhBXZfU4YXNvwPWYBcpKWq w==

" I. All information in possession of any authority, entity, body and agency of the Executive, Legislative and Judicial Powers, autonomous bodies, political parties, trusts and public funds, as well as any individual, moral or union that receives and exercises public resources or perform acts of authority at the federal, state and municipal levels, it is public and may only be temporarily reserved for reasons of public interest and national security, in the terms established by law. In the interpretation of this right, the principle of maximum publicity must prevail. The obligated subjects must document any act that derives from the exercise of their faculties, powers or functions, the law will determine the specific cases under which the declaration of the non-existence of the information will proceed."

In other words, the core petition of the Constitutional Controversy case 214/2018 is based on the National Transparency System, where INAI requires INEGI to reveal statistical information in accordance to article 26, Section B, of the Political Constitution of the United States of Mexico.

According to article 6, clause VIII, fourth paragraph, of the Political Constitution of the United States of Mexico, INAI has jurisdiction to require INEGI to reveal that information:

"

... The guarantor body has competence to hear issues related to access to public information and the protection of personal data of any authority, entity, body or agency that is part of any of the Legislative, Executive and Judicial Powers, autonomous bodies , political parties, trusts and public funds, as well as any individual, moral or trade union that receives and exercises public resources or acts of authority in the federal sphere; with the exception of those jurisdictional matters that correspond to the Supreme Court of Justice of the Nation, in which case a committee composed of three ministers will decide. It shall also be informed of the appeals lodged by the individuals concerning the resolutions of the specialized

autonomous organizations of the federal entities that determine the reservation, confidentiality, non-existence or refusal of the information, in the terms established by law. "

On the other hand, article 26, Section B, of the Political Constitution of Mexico, there is neither special regulation nor restriction on INEGI's jurisdiction because of the fundamental right to Access to public information and that institution is obligated before the National Transparency System to guarantee that right.

Also, the Constituent Reformer did not establish any jurisdiction exceptions or exclusive competency before the National Transparency System, because the essential purpose of consolidating with the Constitutional Reform is to guarantee the fundamental right of Access to public information by all the sources, documents and evidence from the whole institutions that receive public resources.

Notably when neither restriction nor constitutional reserve in article 26, section B, excludes INEGI accomplishment of article 6, Section A, clauses I and VIII, regulations.

Hence, it is inaccurate INEGI's argument where there is no restriction of the fundamental right to Access to public information that must be exercised under exclusive jurisdiction to article 26, section B, through Statistics and Geography Public Service System (claim) when a petitioner shall dispute the content of statistical information.

The Constituent Reformer will stand to only by unicity efforts and practical reason, by INAI, just like the National System gives notice about that competency and INEGI is one more institution of those duties, actions and Transparency directives.

The Reformer gives the legal prescription, to coordinate the System; it is established in article 6, section A, clause VIII, last paragraph, as follows: *"... The guarantor body will coordinate its actions with the Superior Audit Office of the Federation, with the entity specialized in archives and with the body in charge of regulating the collection, processing, and publication of statistical and geographic information, as well as with the guarantor organizations. The federal entities, to strengthen the public accountability of Mexico. "*

According to article 3, clauses VII and XII, of the General Transparency and Public Information Act, the documents that INEGI has in terms of Statistics and Geography National System Act are public information, especially when National Interest Information of statistics and indicators of the Judicial Functions.

In other words, INEGI's information is public information because it is created by Federal Budget resources, especially the National Interest Information, that is public.

For the above reasons, the Constitutional Controversy case *INEGI v. INAI*, must be dismissed by a cause of inadmissibility that empowers the Supreme Court of Justice of the Nation. About that proposition, it applies the decision P./J. 6/2012 (10th Time) from the Plenary of the Supreme Court of Justice of the Nation, available in the Judicial Book of the Federation, book IX, tome 1, page 19, dated June 2012, as follows:

CONSTITUTIONAL CONTROVERSY. THE CHALLENGE OF RESOLUTIONS DICTATED BY THE STATE ORGANS SPECIALIZED IN MATTERS OF ACCESS TO PUBLIC INFORMATION, FOR REASONS OF PURE LEGALITY AND POINT OF CONSIDERATION OF THE PARTICIPATION OF THE COMMUNICATIONS OF THE COMPANY. In accordance with article 25 of the Act of the clauses I and II of Article 105 of the Political Constitution of the United States of Mexico, the Minister of Instruction may be dismissed the plan of the constitutional controversy claim and its annexes warn of a motive manifest and the undoubted inadmissibility, the mode of the evidentiary phase and the answer can not distort it. Therefore, and every occasion, in the Supreme Court of Justice of the Nation, the constitutional controversy has been maintained, not in the proper way to challenge the jurisdictional or analogous character, unless there is a problem of invasion of the spheres if the wording has become a principle of a claim. The matter and how the particular administrative procedure is seen as a corporal as if it were a resource in the later medium of the defense, it is evident that there can be a clear and undoubted motive of inadmissibility that leads to a flat discard the demand.

Now, on August 29, 2018, a petition was formulated before the National Transparency Platform asking INEGI as follows:

"1. I request to know how much is the AVERAGE DURATION OF RESOLUTION OF LEGAL CASES of procedures and processes of civil, commercial, family, criminal, mixed, Teenage, as well as of those that have known in the field of their competence, of the courts in each and every one of the States of the country.

2. I request to know how much is the AVERAGE DURATION OF RESOLUTION OF LEGAL CASES of the jurisdictional processes and procedures processed in Administrative Courts of the States.

3. I request to know how much is the AVERAGE DURATION OF RESOLUTION OF LEGAL CASES of the jurisdictional processes and procedures processed in the Federal Board of Conciliation and Arbitration.

4. I request to know how much is the AVERAGE DURATION OF RESOLUTION OF LEGAL CASES of the jurisdictional processes and procedures processed in the Boards of Conciliation and Arbitration and the Bureaucratic Courts of Conciliation and Arbitration, of the states of the country.

5. I request to know how much is the AVERAGE DURATION OF RESOLUTION OF LEGAL CASES of the jurisdictional processes and procedures processed in the Federal Administrative Court.

6. I request to know how much is the AVERAGE DURATION OF RESOLUTION OF LEGAL CASES of the jurisdictional processes and procedures processed in the Federal Bureaucratic Labor Court.

7. I request to know how much is the AVERAGE DURATION OF RESOLUTION OF LEGAL CASES of the jurisdictional processes and procedures processed in the HIGHER AGRARIAN COURT and the UNITARY AGRARIAN TRIBUNALS of the country. "

The petition was made considering the available information in the National Census of State Justice Administration 2018 and the National Census of Federal Justice Administration 2018, where INEGI calculated the Average Duration of Resolution of Legal Cases (ADRLC).

According to the National Census of Federal Justice Administration 2018, these are the following ADRLC estimates:

- 539 days (CRIMINAL FEDERAL CASE).
- 299 days (CONSTITUTIONAL CASE).
- 280 days (CIVIL AND ADMINISTRATIVE LAW CASE).
- 234 days (AMPARO LAW APPEAL CASE BEFORE SCJN).
- 179 days (NEW SYSTEM COMMERCIAL LAW DISPUTATION).
- 167 days (AMPARO LAW CASE BEFORE CIRCUIT COURT).
- 156 days (AMPARO LAW APPEAL CASE BEFORE CIRCUIT COURT).
- 100 days (APPEAL CASE BEFORE SCJN).
- 96 days (AMPARO LAW CASE BEFORE DISTRICT COURT).
- 57 days (COMPLAINT APPEAL BEFORE CIRCUIT COURT).

Furthermore, in a scientific paper financed by the Bank of Mexico (BANXICO)[57], an estimated timetable is built of knowing the ADRLC with INEGI's data. Therefore, INEGI denies the information.

---

[57] *"Eficiencia del Sistema de Justicia y Desempeño Económico Regional de en México"*, by Juan Carlos Chavez Martín del Campo, Felipe J. Fonseca and Manuel de Jesús Gomez Zaldivar, june 2017, page 14; op cit.16.

The data for commercial disputes in the states of Mexico are 358 days, a national average between 244 and 525 days. Chapter II informs about this useful research.

According to article 17 of the Political Constitution of the United States of Mexico, the core petition to INEGI is to reveal the time that the trials and procedures delay on Mexico. It is convenient to say that INEGI is an expert institution to coordinate the indicators of the whole judicial statistics in each court of the country.

Moreover, its constitutional duty established on article 26, section B, has a strategic utility because statistics and technical information allow making institutional decisions between the Branches of the State. Also, INEGI's data is useful for labor, science, education and culture purposes.

Now, it is essential to say that INEGI has vast data and historical information (at least from 1983) making relevant its institutional duty in the National Transparency System.

For the above reasons, pondering the content of the article 17 of the Political Constitution of the United States of Mexico, it is not credible that an Institution that receives during 2019 Federal Budget $12,000,000,000.00 is either nugatory and unable to reveal a necessary information (ADRLC) in every Court of Mexico, that said, the time that trials and procedures delay.

Neither Constitutional Reform nor Law amendments are promoted without INEGI's information. If don´t, what does INEGI do?

On April 26, 2016, the Conference *"Ordinary Justice dialogues"* was celebrated, concluding more than 16 months of authorities, Courts and institutions collaboration, including three Bar Associations (ANADE, BMA, and INCAAM). In that conference, INEGI participated with statistics and official estimates, as well as the Judicial Branch of the Federation[58].

---

[58] Available in PDF file "DÍALOGOS POR LA JUSTICIA COTIDIANA. DIAGNÓSTICOS CONJUNTOS Y SOLUCIONES" https://www.gob.mx/justiciacotidiana; title "DIÁLOGOS CONJUNTOS Y SOLUCIONES".

Therefore, if there is available data that promotes a Constitutional Reform, as occurred during 2016, it is concluded that INEGI has the required information.

In the resolution of the claim RRA-6844/18, INAI's Plenary decides that INEGI has a National Subsystem of Government, Public Security and Justice Administration, which has statistical information infrastructure that integrates, at least one geo-statistical framework, a national inventory of administrative records, a registry of State Units and a list of Projects and Statistical products that support the obtaining of official information regarding the management and performance of public institutions and the delivery of justice.

The INAI resolved that the INEGI has the information derived from the National Census of State Justice Administration, which is considered as of national interest and the National Census of Federal Justice Administration, that has for generating statistical and geographic information of the Judicial Branch of the Federation, so that it is linked to the governmental work within the process of design, implementation, monitoring, and evaluation of public policies of national scope in the field of justice.

It should be noted that following a series of reforms to the regulatory framework of the National System of Statistical and Geographic Information Act published in the Official Journal of the Federation on June 25, 2018, they were raised to the level of obligation of the National System of Statistical and Geographical Information Act the duties conferred to those subsystems.

As a colophon, the nature of the required information, on December 28, 2012, and September 27, 2016, INEGI's Government Board decided Agreements whereby it considers as National Interest Information that from the National Census of State Justice and Federal Justice Administration.

Hence, if INEGI has vast databases of information since 1983 and actively participates with a public function of expert body in statistics, official information that works to promote constitutional reforms and new regulations, it is logical to assume that the Obligated Authority has the requested information that is the core cause of the Constitutional Controversy case explained.

For these reasons, it is concluded that the ADRLC of all the matters in the country allows guaranteeing the provisions of Article 17 of the Political Constitution of the United States of Mexico for all the people; in addition to that simple premise, generate effectiveness and public accountability by the Justice Administration as a public service in charge of the Public Treasury.

On the other hand, from a liberal, republican and progressive point of view, for what corresponds to judicial statistics and indicators of public function, it is convenient to say that today, 5% of the ADRLC of the whole procedures are revealed, according to the National Census of Federal Justice Administration 2018.

However, 95% of the rest of ADRLC indicators coming the rest of the Federal Courts and the 32 states of Mexico in Civil Law, Family Law, Commercial Law, Labor Law, Administrative Law, Bureaucratic Labor Law, and Agrarian Law, until today, the data are unknown.

For these reasons, the lack of transparency on this public and National Interest generates severe damage to the Rule of Law and the Justice Administration as a public service charged to the Federal Treasury. That omission of the State in providing public information concerning the average duration of resolution causes systemic damage to Transparency and Public Accountability principles and essential components of the fundamental right of access to information.

Certainly the issue that is a matter of dispute between both autonomous constitutional authorities resides in the legitimacy of the State Units and the System Informants for the purposes of design, recruitment, production, updating, organization, processing, integration, compilation, publication, dissemination, and conservation of statistical information of both national interest and public interest.

In that sense, in the claim RRA 1048/18, this legitimacy of the data that make up the National Survey of Access to Public Information and Protection of Personal Data (ENAID) of 2016 is highlighted, in order to obtain in an accessible format, as prescribed by the Transparency regulations. On the other hand, in the claim RRA 1676/18, that legitimacy is found in the information consisting of the database that justifies the "*Census, Teachers and Students of Basic and Special Education 2013*

(CEMABE) - Format F-911 ", Prepared in coordination with INEGI and the Ministry of Public Education, by mandate of the Educational Reform of 2013, belonging to the Educational Information and Management System.

Finally, in resolution RRA 8592/18, that legitimacy concerns the Social Cohesion Survey for the Prevention of Violence and Crime (ECOPRED) 2014, regarding the inconsistent and diverse information required.

For the foregoing and for the good of Mexico, the public information that corresponds to the average duration of resolution of cases that the National Institute of Statistics and Geography, INEGI must provide, must be disclosed.

Notwithstanding the foregoing, it is important to say that, at the close of the second edition, more than 300 days had been delayed since the Constitutional Dispute started before the Plenary of the Supreme Court of Justice of the Nation on 23 November 2018, while the various correlated 117/2018 exceeds 365 calendar days. Constitutional case 9/2019 is still in the process of integration.

V.   Discoveries and Legal Sabermetrics: prospective.

Revealing the situation of the Justice Administration in Mexico has made it possible to discover a series of essential data for Public Accountability, Transparency and Access to information by Courts and Prosecutors of the country.

Next, by questions and answers, discoveries and suggestions that are considered relevant for the future of the country are presented.

a. What is the conceptual framework of Judicial Statistics in Mexico?

According to the analysis and the research of more than 200 Obligated Authorities that provide information on their functions, competencies, and faculties in a disaggregated manner, there is a complete discretion with the handling of statistical data to publicize at the convenience the situation those organs of justice throughout the country keep.

That is, each authority collects, processes constructs its judicial statistics because of their policies, and traditional customs, in some cases in a conventional manner, because it is easy to disclose, either in a primary way or in complexity.

Therefore, this discovery (*problem*) is due to the lack of a basic conceptual framework of judicial statistics that allows, in a simple and intelligible way, to analyze the functions, faculties, and competences regarding the matters that are promoted from both the Federation and the 32 states each year under the Budget expenditures.

Pondering the analyzed cases, the suggestion that I propose is processing the judicial statistics in a primary structure due to the fiscal year in turn to measure the effectiveness of the institutions.

The basic conceptual framework of judicial statistics is as follows:

The basic conceptual framework of Judicial Statistics				
Pending cases	Received cases	Concluded cases	Process cases	Litigation amount
It relates to the pending lawsuits of previous fiscal years; initial inventory or existence.	It refers to admitted claims and judicial prosecution, considering any concept of entry.	It refers to matters entered that obtain a final judgment, an extrajudicial conclusion, or apply a specific outcome for the time.	It refers to the difference between issues entered, plus the laggards, less the cases concluded at the end of the fiscal year.	Economic amount of the controversies

From this basic framework, it can be developed any disaggregation degree into complexity to detect the real aspects of the Justice Administration during a fiscal year, understanding that the response to the complexity of disaggregation is consistent, with technological tools and judicial information techniques of data mining that reveal the simplicity of Public Accountability. Future research will focus on analyzing the empirical basis by which current judicial statistics and data collection mechanisms are produced.

In any case both, State Units and the System informants, according to the Statistical and Geographical Information Act, are those that define the fidelity of the information and the reliability of the same, for purposes of complying with statistical principles.

Hence, if a State Unit or System Informant conceals, denies or manipulates the information, the statistical product will be futile.

b. How Mexico's Court's efficacy is measured?

According to the analyzed information in Chapter II and III, we discovered that the Judicial Branch of the Federation, the Supreme Court of Justice of the States of Mexico, the Federal Administrative Court and some of the Administrative Courts and the Board of Conciliation and Arbitration of the states, all these courts have a whole statistical disaggregation as the Basic Conceptual Framework revealed, so its effectiveness can be measured during one fiscal year.

The concept that is useful to measure the capacity to provide justice is the **Real Institutional Capacity of Legal Case Resolution** (RICLCRE); its definition is *the set of budgetary, human, material and institutional resources to provide justice and solve legal problems within the scope of their functions, faculties, and competencies during a fiscal year.*

RICLCRE is expressed by the utility of the Basic Conceptual Framework of Judicial Statistics. Technically, RICLCRE can be demonstrated as follows:

$$\frac{\textit{Concluded cases from the fiscal year}}{\textit{Received cases of the fiscal year + Pending cases from the previous fiscal year.}} = \text{RICLCRE}$$

On Chapter II, number 8, *Judicial Statistics (2018 summary)*, we find that the RICLCRE is 42.81%, that is, **for every ten received cases, four are concluded, and six remain pending.** In the Judicial Branch of the Federation, the proportion is 7 out of 10 (*75.00%*) while in the State Courts of 32 states is 2 out of 10 (*24.42%*).

c. How much money is lost due to the lack of efficacy of the Justice Administration?

If we calculate the RICLCRE, we find out an objective reality and a hidden one. The latter is truly important because of a progressive parameter to RICLCRE data.

Then, the Judicial Branch of the Federation and the Supreme Court of Justice of the 32 states of Mexico, plus the Federal Administrative Court, the Administrative State Court and the Labor Boards, have a consolidated Budget between the Federal and the 32 states Treasury of $100,000,000,000.00 (at least) for each fiscal year.

According to RICLCRE, pending cases generate an institutional loss to the Treasury because of the *hidden amount of the binary probability* that complements the effectiveness value. During 2018, RICLCRE was estimated in 42.81%, so the hidden value of the binary probability that complements that effectiveness is 57.19%.

Therefore, the estimate of Institutional Budget Loss due to pending cases generates to the Justice Administration during 2018 in Mexico's Justice Administration is $ 57,190, 000,000.00.

Institutional Budget Loss by pending cases
$57,190,000,000.00

d. Are the lawyers of the Executive Federal Branch eficient?

According to the research, in 18 years of administrative litigation before the Federal Administrative Court, it is noticed that the attorneys of the Federal Public Administration Entities lost 72.43% directly contended disputes, that is, 41,648 out of 57,497 cases. Of those defeats, it is calculated a historical loss to the public treasury of at least $ 448, 606, 069,500.00.

The investigation does not reveal a real factor of recovery in terms of the tax reviews cases before the Circuit Courts of the Judicial Branch of the Federation and the disaggregated resolution.

In accordance with this inoperativeness, the lack of involvement by the Office of the Legal Counsel of the President of Mexico in criminal law cases during the period from January 1, 2001, to January 23, 2019; as the answer of the Transparency Unit of the Office of the Attorney General of the Republic explains, highlights that the legal interests of the Federal Executive Branch have been subject to a deficient legal representation (0 out of 0 cases).

Finally, but without being part of the Federal Executive Power, it draws attention to the institutional effectiveness of an obligated authority that received a consolidated budget of $ 20 billion during the last 19 years. According to the information revealed by the obligated party, the National Human Rights Commission (CNDH) issued 931 recommendations out of 121,622 cases that received, that is, 0.7654%, so that a historic loss to the public treasury of at least $ 19 846, 920, 000.00 can be concluded by protecting human rights.

The investigation does not pronounce on the Human Rights Commissions of the 32 states of Mexico; however, the data of its counterpart, at the federal level, suggests that its role is equally inoperative charged to the Public Treasury.

e. How much corruption is generated by the Justice Administration omission to provide justice?

The existence of a **binary hidden scale of corruption** (BHSC) is proposed as an estimate from the unknown value of RICLCRE in Mexico and the litigation economic amount charged to the Public Treasury during one fiscal year.

The BHSC estimate stands in two propositions: one, corruption produced in courts generates a Treasury loss and two, that illegal activity has an economic value equal to tax evasion.

To calculate the BHSC estimate, the litigation economic amount charged to the Federal Budget must be calculated in 2018, as well as the 32 states Budgets.

Therefore, Chapter II and III proof that before the Federal Administrative Court, in 2018, there was a litigation economic amount of $619, 365,000,000.00.

Considering the coordinated tax System and the dependence to Federal Budget resources by the 32 states of Mexico, the **BHSC estimate is $354, 214, 843,500.00 in 2018**.

Pondering other illegal activities, that economic amount represents up to 6 times the gasoline theft through PEMEX's Critical Infrastructure during a fiscal year.

In any case, the BHSC estimate is calculated because of the Institutional omission of Mexico to provide and to administrate justice according to article 17 of the Political Constitution of the United States of Mexico.

Finally, the BHSC estimate works progressively in respect to RICLCRE: **while greater RICLCRE exists in the justice administration, less corruption will be generated in the system. Logically, lower RICLCRE, greater corruption.**

In any case, it is important to mention that the phenomenon of judicial corruption follows the string of various criminal cabinet or "white collar" phenomena, such as the issuance of tax receipts from non-existent operations or instrumental companies. In this regard, it is important to mention that the Tax Administration Service (SAT) determined that *phantom* companies cause losses to the Treasury for $ 354 billion pesos[59].

f. How long the trials delay?

According to the information revealed in chapters II and III, the ADRLC has made up a correlation of the time lapse of the disputes of each of the Obligated Authorities. Thus, some courts have a disaggregated assessment of the duration of

---

[59] EMPRESAS FANTASMA PROVOCAN PÉRDIDAS AL FISCO POR 354 MIL MDP, SEÑALA EL SAT, El Financiero Bloomberg, 25 de junio del 2019, available in https://www.elfinanciero.com.mx/economia/empresas-fachada-provocan-perdidas-al-fisco-por-354-mil-mdp-senala-el-sat

their affairs, such as in the Judicial Branch of the Federation, the Supreme Court of Justice of Mexico City, Nuevo Leon, and Administrative State Courts.

The information revealed in this essay shows that the fact of assessing the ADRLC requires, first, a basic conceptual framework of judicial statistics, and then, to have a tool, instrument, algorithm or a real-time disaggregation technique in order to monitor during a fiscal year the information produced by the country's justice administration bodies regarding the duration of the litigation.

Now, on BANXICO's research paper, the authors consider that "...*If judicial decisions take too much time, these would have an immediate impact on the normal operation of a company, since they may not have sufficient capital to finance their normal operations or invest in new development projects. Also, the absence of confidence in the judicial power could make companies limit themselves to doing business with trusted suppliers or clients, already known, which would reduce the probability of finding better business opportunities with new companies[60].*"

BANXICO's scientists arrived through several equations and Open Source Data from INEGI, CONAPO and World Bank to calculate the ADRLC of commercial law disputes. However, the revealed problem in this book exposes the pending legal cases in Federal and States of Mexico jurisdictions in all the topics with more than 20 years in a legal dispute; so that the ADRLC is a dynamic indicator of Public Accountability to supervise the Justice Administration.

Unless your best opinion, article 17 of the Political Constitution of the United States of Mexico establishes that *every person has the right to be administered justice by courts that will be expedited to impart it within the terms set by law, issuing their resolutions of prompt, complete and impartial manner. The service will be free; therefore, court costs are forbidden.*

So, *how much time will be enough to receive justice in Mexico?*

To satisfy this argument, a basic conceptual framework to calculate the ADRLC is proposed as follows:

---

[60] Op. Cit. 17. Page. 4.

Date of Judicial Start	Date of resolution.	Number of days to resolution.	Definitive File.	Number of days to Definitive File.
ADRLC (CONSOLIDATED AVERAGE)			AVERAGE DURATION OF CONCLUSION	
AVERAGE DURATION OF CASES				

g. When does the problem of pending legal cases date?

According to the analysis realized and the available information, considering the pending labor law, civil law and criminal law cases in the 32 states of Mexico, we can assume that a general problem preexists in the Justice Administration since 50 years ago (at least).

h. How many legal cases does the Administration of President Andres Manuel Lopez Obrador have?

Through a process of compartmentalization of data by the research lines carried out and the analysis of the available statistical information, the following consolidated estimates are obtained:

FEDERAL PUBLIC ADMINISTRATION LEGAL CASES		
CONSOLIDATED ESTIMATES		
TOPIC	**CASES**	**PERCENTAGE**
CONSTITUTIONAL LAW(1)	297,322	38.86%
CIVIL LAW/ ADMINISTRATIVE LAW	365	0.05%
CRIMINAL LAW (2)	67,896	8.87%
BUREAUCRATIC LABOR LAW	26,308	3.44%
LABOR LAW (3)	274,038	35.82%
CNDH- HUMAN RIGHTS	4630	0.61%

ADMINISTRATIVE LAW	64,363	8.41%
AGRARIAN LAW	32	0.00%
INTERNATIONAL HUMAN RIGHTS	13,151	1.72%
IMPORTANT CJEF****	16,979	2.22%
TOTAL	765,084	100.00%
(1)ESTIMATE CONSIDERING CASES BEFORE SCJN, AMPARO LAW CASES BEFORE DISTRICT COURT AND CIRCUIT COURT, INCLUDING APPEALS, CLAIM, AND INCIDENTS, <CASES BY 75% RICLCRE DURING 2018>		
(2) INCLUDING APPEALS		
(3) CONSIDERING 63% PENDING CASES BEFORE FEDERAL BOARD OF CONCILIATION AND ARBITRATION		
***NATIONAL ESTIMATES DO NOT CONSIDER TCJS AND NCJS CRIMINAL CASES OF THE ATTORNEY GENERAL OF THE REPUBLIC.		
****CONSIDERING CIADI WORLD BANK CASES.		

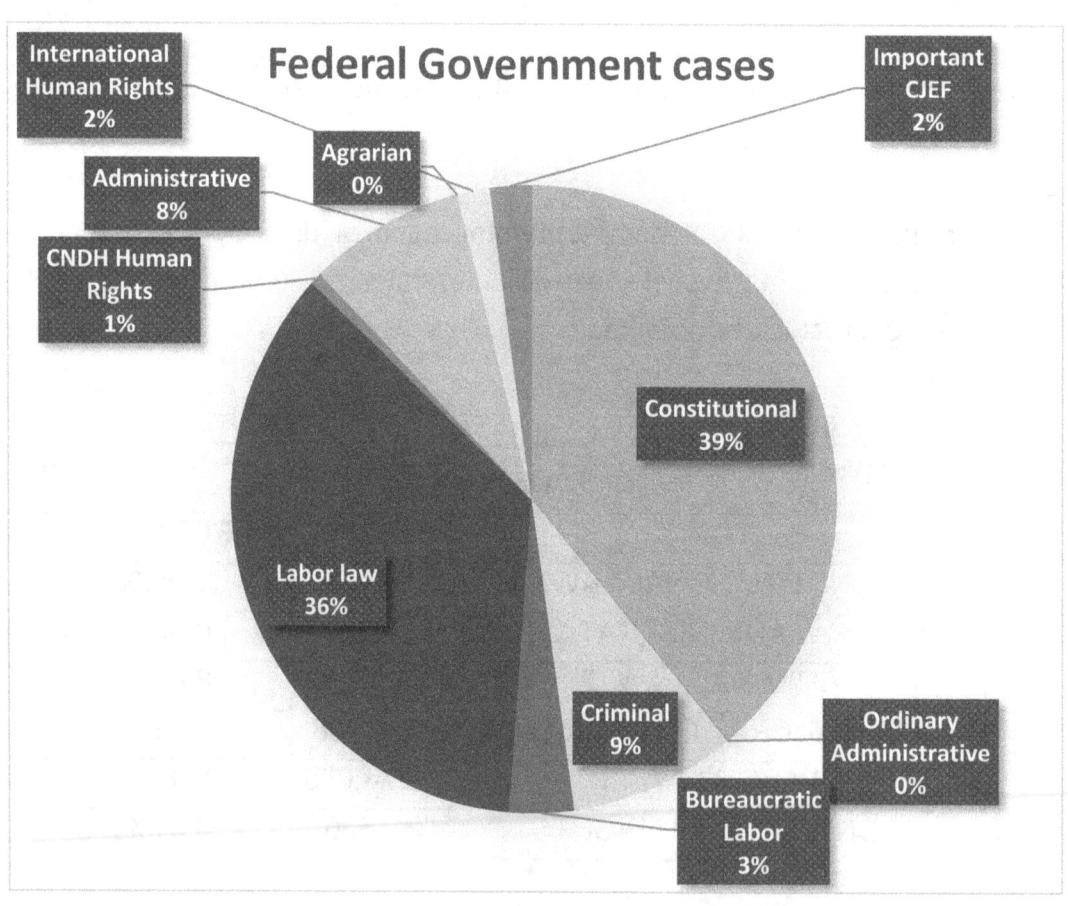

Federal Government cases

International Human Rights 2%
Important CJEF 2%
Agrarian 0%
Administrative 8%
CNDH Human Rights 1%
Constitutional 39%
Labor law 36%
Criminal 9%
Ordinary Administrative 0%
Bureaucratic Labor 3%

i. Are the Departments of the Federal Government attending their issues to provide justice?

According to the research, the information contained in at least nine claims before the Transparency Regulator INAI, (22.5% of all complaints) highlights the lack of attention to the legal matters of the Federal Government, the lack of transparency in the information requested and the lack of Public accountability through statistics to make decisions.

In any case, in a reasonableness judgment, the public administration provides, to the extent of its powers, faculties, functions, and capacities, the information it knows or makes itself known, but the problem of rendering accounts is older than the time the present Administration has been in charge.

j. How many pending cases do exist in Mexico?

The diagnosis of the second edition corroborates a very important fact regarding judicial statistics in Mexico: **the official information of the Courts is manipulable and, therefore, unreliable**.

First, the lack of statistical control under the principles Custody Chain and Statistical Secret of the State Units and their System Informants implies the existence of inconsistencies based on the Official Census.

In this case, we can corroborate these premises through the 2018 and 2019 State Justice Procurement Censuses, where in the first statistical exercise, 167,853 previous inquiries appear pending cases and then, despite the existence of the New Criminal Justice System, the figure amounts to 280,448 cases, stating that several State Units related to Prosecutors of Justice disagree with the figures in both fiscal years.

We can mention the Office of the Attorney General of Mexico City, which, in the first statistical exercise (2018), reveals 0 pending previous inquiries and, in the subsequent subsequent one (2019), amounts to 12,575 cases, notwithstanding that, between both statistical exercises, the official lag has increased by 521.47%, from 28,367 pending cases to 147,927.

Another diverse event of statistical discrepancy and unreliability is found in the State Justice Impartion Census 2018 and 2019. For example, in the State of Mexico, during 2018, 74,000 pending cases were reported, while in the year 2019, 711,284 cases appear , that is, 961.19% increase.

Notwithstanding the foregoing, it is pertinent to say that, according to the collection of petitions to more than 200 obliged subjects, it follows that the number of pending cases is much higher than the various official estimates by the constitutional body autonomous, despite its capacity for financial, human, material and budgetary resources.

As it has been exposed and verified throughout this book, the lack of a disaggregated judicial statistic of Courts according to a basic conceptual framework that reveals the Public Accountability of these Obligated Authorities represent a significant institutional omission that impacts on the Public Treasury of the Federal Government and the states of Mexico.

According to the research, a considerable number of pending cases has been discovered, well above the official figures INEGI and the Courts disaggregated statistical records reveal. The task has been in a temporary frame of at least 20 years, and the results have led to dating records with more than 50 years of dispute.

On chapter II, this book incorporated an initial summary of public information available from Official Censuses and institutional websites.

Next, a summary of estimates regarding the consolidated, disaggregated and investigated information throughout this document consisting of the matters that exist in the Courts of the 32 states, Administrative, Bureaucratic Labor and Labor law cases, as well as the Attorney General's Offices throughout the country, is presented.

To reach the estimates, the total number of revealed matters is taken into account and multiplied by the hidden factor with respect to the revealed factor, which consists of the percentage of favorable answers obtained between the number of states plus the federation in its consolidated (33) for each disaggregated, whether in labor, bureaucratic labor, administrative, civil and criminal law topics.

At the end of this book, in Chapter VII, consolidated national numbers are presented.

The jurisdictional estimates that are calculated at the beginning of the spring of 2019 are the following:

PENDING CASES NATIONAL ESTIMATES					
JURISDICTION	REVEALED CASES	% REVEALED (1)	% HIDDEN DATA (2)	DIFFERENCE (3)	PENDING CASES ESTIMATES.
Labor cases	915,765	60.60%	39.40%	360,811.41	1,276,576.41
Bureaucratic Labor cases	82,979	42.42%	57.58%	47,779.31	130,758.31
Supreme Court of Justice of the 32 states pending cases	3,814,049	60.60%	39.40%	1,502,535.31	5,316,584.31
Administrative cases	135,365	90.90%	9.10%	12,318.22	147,683.22
Pending Judicial Branch of the Federation	464,325	100.00%	0.00%	0.00	464,325.00
Agrarian cases	49,900	100.00%	0.00%	0.00	49,900.00
States Attorney General.	2,963,593	33.33%	66.67%	1,975,827.45	4,939,420.45
TOTAL (5)	8,425,976	69.69%	30.31%	3,899,271.70	12,325,247.70
(1) REVEALED PETITIONS/ 33 (STATES + FEDERAL GOVERNMENT)					

(2) BINARY HIDDEN DATA TO REVEAL THE PERCENTAGE.
(3) RESEARCH CASES BY BINARY DATA TO REVEAL INFORMATION
(4) VALUE IS OBTAINED BY THE HIDDEN REVELATION NUMBER BY THE REVEALED CASES PLUS THE NUMBER OF REVEALED CASES.
(5) REVEALED CASES;

Regarding these estimates, according to the statistical support of the second edition book, with a total disclosure of 83%, a degree of accuracy of 97.42% of these values was found, **which verifies the fidelity of the instrument used by binary method (see chapter VII APPENDIX).**

However, it is pertinent to mention a statistical phenomenon detected during the work and that will serve the reader to simplify the understanding of the national problem, in the right dimension that must be weighted.

It is true that the figures consolidated here were obtained thanks to research work in more than 200 organs of law enforcement and prosecution that lead to the discretion of the statistical management of their functions, faculties and competences. Therefore, it is pertinent to mention that the figures handled not even INEGI in more than 35 years have consolidated a work of such complexity, despite the obligations inherent in articles 6 and 26, section B, of the Political Constitution of the States United Mexicans, in terms of transparency and accountability.

For these reasons, it is certainly too annoying and, in addition, incredible, that a constitutional authority that stores state infrastructure to carry out this kind of exercise lacks the leadership and sense of public service to obtain the truthful information with which decisions are made by the State.

Regardless of this sovereign vicissitude (not to say dysplicity), in the investigated universe of judicial data in Mexico, we can appreciate the disaggregation of the data from a principle called **SCALE FROM ONE (1) TO TEN (10),** pondering the number of trials and criminal matters pending resolution regarding the number of inhabitants residing in Mexico.

Under this *principle*, we can find that the number of inhabitants at the date of data collection was more than 123 million people during the spring of the year 2019, so, according to the empirical approaches, we can obtain that verification.

1 TO 10 SCALE	
12,325,247.70 PENDING CASES DURING SPRING OF 2019	10% PROPORTION
MORE THAN 123 MILLION PEOPLE IN MEXICO	

So, to simplify the topical understanding of the phenomenon of disaggregation of national estimates, we find it distributed between the number of trials and current criminal investigations. In the case analyzed, from the universe of 12, 325,247.70 pending cases, we found at least 4,939,420.45 criminal investigations in the country, representing a total of 40.07% of the estimated universe, while a remaining 59.93% of cases are constricted to trials, whether in constitutional, civil, commercial, labor, administrative, bureaucratic and criminal matters.

By way of rational belief and approximating the percentages to the nearest unit, in Mexico, we can present a 60-40 proportion with respect to that estimated universe of pending issues that exist in the country.

PENDING CASES PROPORTION	
60% TRIALS	40% CRIMINAL INVESTIGATIONS

In any case, if there are major issues to the estimates proposed here, there would be a severe state problem regarding the RICRLC that it can execute through all financial, human, material and budgetary resources, which should not be ruled out due to the systemic weaknesses of judicial statistical information at the national level.

Finally, I consider it appropriate to say that forecast the management of the variables of RICRLC and ADRLC for subsequent fiscal years in a chaotic universe of statistical information, as is the case in Mexico, is too complex, if not idle and harmful.

In a different forecast used thanks to the National Census in the Superior Courts of Justice, where more than 40% of the total judicial lag is found, we find a variation of entries and concluded cases as follows:

ENTRIES-CONCLUDED CASES VARIATION	
ENTRIES (ON THE RISE)	CONCLUDED (DOWNWARD)
2.44% to 3.8%	5.51% to 6.1%

For the reasons stated and, in practical terms, as long as there is no authentic handling of statistical information by INEGI and the State Units of all courts and prosecutors of the country through a uniform conceptual framework, I suggest using these estimates so that in any case, a statistical exercise similar to what was done in this book during the spring of the year 2025 is prepared, in order to complete a more in-depth analysis of what is currently obtained.

k. How many pending cases have more than 20 years of disputation?

According to the revealed data by the Supreme Court of Justice of the states of Aguascalientes, Coahuila, Guerrero, Michoacan, and Tamaulipas, a consolidated average of 1.05% pending cases with more than 20 years of litigation is calculated.

See the following figures:

Consolidated time litigation			
State	Cases Before Dec. 31, 1999	TOTAL	% (Final Average)
Aguascalientes	2,652	125,332	2.12%
Michoacan	1572	102,801	1.53%
Guerrero	622	211,880	0.29%

Coahuila	1217	99,896	1.22%
Tamaulipas	30	33,945	0.09%
TOTAL	6,093	573,854	1.05%

Now, according to the consolidated national estimate before the Supreme Court of Justice of the 32 states, it is calculated that 1.05% of the whole pending cases (5, 316,584.31) have more than 20 years of disputation, that is, **55,824.13 cases**.

Labor law estimate is calculated by 0.82% of the national universe (1, 276, 576.41), with the same time delay, **10,580.80 cases**.

Generally, we consider **66,408.93** pending cases with more than 20 years of dispute.

I. How many political prisoners are in Mexico?

This research reveals the existence of criminal cases that have been pending for more than ten years before the Federal Courts and the 32 state Courts. Under these circumstances, a criminal case that has more than ten years without any resolution is considered *a political prisoner*.

Therefore, according to the available information, there are 26,716 pending criminal cases before Federal Courts from April 2, 2001, to December 31, 2009[61]. On the other side, the State of Guerrero has 23,641[62] pending criminal cases; the State of Jalisco has 49,244[63] and the State of Michoacan 4,548[64] pending cases.

The data of this investigation yield **104,149 political prisoners pending cases with more than one decade of criminal litigation without resolution of their disputes**, an estimated 52.05% of all criminal cases in the country.

---

[61] 25893 criminal cases and 826 appeals.

[62] 235 criminal cases before December 31, 1999 and 23,406 from 2000-2010.

[63] 29,854 criminal cases, 10,201 foreign criminal cases and 9,189 criminal mix.

[64] 646 criminal cases before December 31, 1999 and 3902 cases from January 1, 2000 to December 31, 2010.

m. What the states of Mexico have more pending cases?

In the first edition of this book, according to the investigation carried out and with the revealed data of the Judicial Power of each entity, Labor Boards, Bureaucracy Court, Administrative Court and Attorney General's Office, the top 5 jurisdictions with major issues pending and pending resolution are the State of Nuevo León (1,336,396), the State of Jalisco (1,258,466), the Federation (1,039,877), Mexico City (598, 453) and the State of Baja California (588,963). The 5 that follow are the State of Michoacan (514,636), State of Mexico (479,774), State of Puebla (454,723), State of Sonora (348,752) and the State of Yucatan (216,495).

Subsequently and thanks to the *high card method*, the top 5 lag is consolidated in Mexico City (1,495, 243), the Federation (1, 339,877), Nuevo León (1, 339,598), Jalisco (1, 258,466) and the State of Mexico (919,280), representing 53.22% of the entire consolidated national lag.

Notwithstanding the foregoing, it is pertinent to say that, due to the institutional weakness for the purpose of forming judicial statistics, these figures may vary.

n. Do new regulations and constitutional reforms to develop new legal models generate efficacy?

The revealed data exposes that constitutional reforms and new regulations implemented and spread propagandistically to the Legal Forum had produced a legal paradox: *instead of providing the resolution of legal cases, the constitutional changes and new rules have detonated the obsolescence and inoperability of the Justice Administration, regardless of the preexistence of the pending legal cases problem.*

As we can see from the Census conducted by INEGI from 2016 to 2019, there is a paradox regarding the institutional capacity to solve legal problems: **the same value of RICRLC has been lost. with respect to the initially measured for said value.**

While in the 2016 Census the RICRLC for the federative entities it amounted to more than 38.05%, in 2019 it is 23.36%, which means that it was reduced by 38.61% at that time, exceeding the same initially calculated value.

This means that the State has squandered the same number of resources destined to impart justice regarding what it can effectively deal with in a residual way, therefore, these reforms can be corroborated.

If we analyze it in monetary terms, if 30% of the consolidated budget for the Administration of Justice is of the Superior Courts of Justice and at least $ 90 billion pesos have been allocated in the last 3 fiscal years, we will find that the federal entities have lost more than $ 38 billion pesos in the last three years due to this detrimental dynamics for the total amount allocated to the higher courts of justice, which is equally proportional or higher than that allocated in a consolidated fiscal year.

Hence, the fact of creating regulations or amending them, or promoting constitutional reforms, is a cosmetic decision or pure marlakey.

o. When did the problem of pending cases of the Justice Administration start to get worse than ever?

According to the analyzed and revealed data, the problem has its genesis in 2008, at the beginning of the implementation of the Constitutional Reforms of the New Criminal Justice System (NCJS), as well as Human Rights and Amparo Law reforms, due to the lack of consolidated statistical information system in Mexico that realizes the situation of the Justice Administration, where the functions, faculties, and competencies disaggregated by the Public Treasury are stated; that is, how much do I solve with charge to Budget.

Other possible generating causes may be the budgetary distortion due to the exponential increase of the Federal Judicial Branch as a result of the previously announced constitutional reforms, which affected the rest of the Courts in their RICLCRE by a Budget Proportion 2 to 1, when the Courts of the 32 states, including Administrative and Labor Courts, lead the solution of conflicts preponderantly.

Another possibility is the exercise and implementation of public policies in the organs of justice of the states to concentrate with the budgetary resources all the institutional efforts in the implementation of the constitutional reforms, losing sight of the attention of pending cases until the date of the beginning of its validity.

p. How many Courts are still using manual and printed data collection systems to produce judicial statistics?

According to the available information and the statistical analysis, it can be estimated that most of the Statistics Systems data in Mexico is produced and collected manually, as well as a simple Archive system to keep the control of the legal information.

The Federal Judiciary Council and the Federal Administrative Court systems, as well as the Supreme Court of Justice of Mexico City, the Judicial Branch of the State of Nuevo Leon and the Labor Boards of the State of Guanajuato systems, have a significant technological advancement.

Also, the States of Morelos, Jalisco, Campeche, and Michoacan produce their judicial statistics by disaggregated parameters to complexity, as well as Open Data tools management.

This book does not reveal the implementation of Intelligent Systems/ Artificial Intelligence by functions related to judicial statistics on real-time among the Courts of Mexico.

In the same way, this research does NOT pronounce on statistical audit processes, beyond the inaccuracies detected, due to the systemic weaknesses of the institutional information.

q. What can we do to solve the problem of Mexico's Justice Administration?

The first diagnosis (*suggested*) that can be arrived at when analyzing the information in this book consists of the implementation of a Constitutional Reform to the Justice Administration by creating Auxiliary Courts of the Federation, with concurrent jurisdiction in coordinated themes to the 32 states of Mexico through

Transitional Justice, in order to solve pending cases in a finite period of time. That is, to promote a constitutional reform due to public necessity so that the Federation regains control of the controversies in a concurrent and subsidiary manner, starting from the Federal Budget dependence.

To achieve the core goal, the first strategy suggestion is to establish 32 Auxiliary Super Tribunals of the Federation with Super Judges that have amplified functions to Due Process of Law and mixed-concurrent jurisdiction, to solve 12 million pending cases through a transitional justice scheme during one decade of resolution, at least.

We consider 7 Super Judges with a basic structure of 1 Super General Clerk of the Court that will take the integration of cases and the regularization of the trials; 7 Clerks for each Super Judge with faculties to supply functions of trial judges to amplify the institutional capacity, 30 judicial actuaries and 90 official clerks, to have a sufficient alignment that can support during the defined period of time (10 years) the constitutional duty to solve the pending cases here narrated in civil, criminal, labor, bureaucratic labor and administrative law cases, through rotating functions and concurrent work schemes.

In that transitional justice canon, a "logical" proposal would be the reduction of the Supreme Court of Justice of the Nation from 11 to 7 Justices, and the redistribution of 40% of its operational personnel, middle ranks and Clerks in judicial functions of said Auxiliary Court of the Federation, especially when the highest paid public officials are those who work in the Supreme Court of Justice of the Nation and resolve less than the rest of the country's justice courts. The Mexican taxpayer pays for an overly expensive Constitutional Court, away from society and with a bad public reputation.

In the same guise of the useless, certainly the elimination of the Federal Judiciary Council, the administrative bureaucracy of that Branch of the Union, and its administrative and budgetary redistribution to the Federal Entities would simplify the diagnosis of judges of those super Auxiliary Court of the Federation.

However, the feasibility of creating these 32 Auxiliary Courts depends on the Federal Budget, which would mean a public investment of at least $60 billion per year to create an identically effective structure to the Judicial Branch of the Federation in its 75.00% RICLCRE, to attend 1 million cases per year, which is complicated as impossible in budgetary terms. In addition to the above, the fact that pending cases generate an annualized fiscal loss, as has been demonstrated, makes it ambiguous to invest public money to waste it.

Similarly, it should be noted that the process of this Constitutional Reform, without budgetary optimization will generate a more profound problem to tropicalize a new system by just propaganda, despite the fact being either cosmetic and malarkey.

Now, the reforms and legal amendments currently proposed in the Congress of the Union, including the new Federal Labor Act and its labor transition process, are aimed at deepening the problem described, not because of the symbolic fact of its guarantors ideas and institutions, but that, in the objective level of the RICLCRE before Courts of the 32 states of Mexico, **it will be paid with almost 800,000 additional pending cases to the more than 5 million cases that currently exist**, that it would be an impossible paradox to solve, estimating a total of six million pending legal cases to solve at the moment in which the labor transition to Labor Courts takes place.

Therefore, *What can we do with the shortage of Public Resources and the Historical problem exposed as pure Evil, one that wastes our money and generates corruption in Courts?*

According to *legal sabermetrics*, the first solution is purely statistical and by administrative control through Judicial Visitator and Institutional purge. It is estimated that, among the 11 million pending cases, 25% of them can be filed definitively by the expiration of the case or prescription. In these cases, it is foreseeable the existence either extinct or "burned" cases with the time that has prevailed through corrupted methods and bribery to reduce the justiciability and procedural fairness, so this measure is properly disciplinary by administrative within the organs of justice of the whole country.

A similar strategy is feasible in criminal cases considering statistical behavior-patterns in high-impact crimes by disaggregated data from temporary files and definitive files, to gather evidence to attack at least 20% of the criminal cases that could be investigated. However, this task requires the implementation of statistical data mining and intelligent technology in the Attorney General's Offices to constitute AI technology, for which public investment in this point is mandatory.

Another simple solution is to enable the Courts and Tribunals that receive fewer cases to the rest of the average of the Courts, such as Criminal Justice Centers, Administrative Units of the Supreme Court of Justice of the 32 states of Mexico; the Electoral Court of the Judicial Branch of the Federation, the Administrative Units of the Federal Judiciary Council, as well as the Legal Culture Houses of the Supreme Court of Justice of the Nation, in order to keep an objective functionality of priority attention of controversies. That is, to use what is available and preponderantly used in an isolated and auxiliary by cultural or social activities, to undertake the actual problem.

In addition to these proposals, another simple solution and does not require more than a simple modification to the Organic Acts of the Judicial Branch of the States, as well as the institutional will on the part of their Supreme Court of Justice of the 32 states and the Federal Judiciary Council itself, is to enable Magistrates and Unitary Auxiliary Courts, as well as Clerks whose statistical performance is lower with respect to the cases known to other judges, by solidarity functions and subsidiary way, to settle in court the affairs of their peers. Of course, the only regulation cause that is suggested to safeguard is the Judicial Disqualification (*impediment*).

Another proposal, (complex) of those that sabermetrically have been suggested stands in generating budgetary balance and equity to increase the resources of the Consolidated Budget for the Justice Administration. Indeed, the Supreme Courts of Justice of the States, the Labor Boards and the Administrative Courts operate in budgetary discrimination for the functions that exist at the federal level; the budgets of the Federal Administrative Court, Federal Bureaucratic Court, and Higher Agrarian Court are managed to budget availability in each fiscal year.

Moreover, an equitable proposal would be to generate a proportional increase between 100 and 200% for the Judicial Branches of the 32 states and courts where there is more considerable, through a scheme of budgetary contributions at the federal level to serve it. However, it is reiterated: the proposal is complicated because, in terms of Federal Budget, its design and implementation have priorities that the Federal Congress realizes according to The Power of the Purse and The Appropriations.

Now, the genuinely crucial topic is the case of the Attorney General of the 32 states of Mexico, since the consolidation of the New Criminal Justice System has permanent monitoring and follow-up that points to the lack of legal actions to promote litigation and solve the problems revealed in this book. One possibility is to enable the figure of the "private investigator" or "coadjutants" to investigate criminal cases. However, this topic can be considered either trivial and paradoxical.

In addition to these proposals, the function that is obsolete and useless at the moment regarding the destination of Public resources for the Justice Administration, to the extent that a reinvention is suggested, the National Commission of Human Rights, an institution that has infrastructure, material resources, human resources and sufficient legal training to do more than simple recommendatory papers, and to promote human rights actions of a propagandist or advertising nature, when its institutional role with respect to the data nowadays they exist in international instances, they highlight their futility as a State option.

A sudden discovery of the research on the role of the CNDH stands in its prospective as a Public Defender of the People who will litigate, help and solve the old problems revealed in civil, family, commercial, criminal, labor, bureaucratic labor, and agrarian law cases. Therefore, the institutional role will change direction in the 32 states with each Human Rights institution, managing an estimated budget of $3.00 billion per year.

Therefore, **the solution is not about lack of public money, but about its cognitive application to what works or to what is useful, focusing on what works and ruling out the inoperative**. If money is mandatory, well, money is there, but invested to futile functions and faculties, and obsolete competences.

For these reasons, as a legal sabermetric discovery in prospective, an estimate of at least $60 billion, misused, can be redirected to bring resolution to the actual problem:

JUSTICE ADMINISTRATION BUDGET REFORM			
LEGAL SABERMETRICS STRATEGIES			
Jurisdiction	Budget Loss	Objective	Budget Investment
Courts	-$57.19	Auxiliarly Courts of the Federation	$57.19
CNDH and 32 states Human Rights institutions	-$2.81	Public Defender of the People	$2.81
TOTAL	-$60.00	-	$60.00
Numbers in Billion.			

The more actions are carried out in order to solve this historical problem through those effective institutions, the higher the probability that in our country the principles of peace and social stability will prevail, as well as the recovery of the rational belief and confidence in the institutions that administer justice, remembering that 230 years ago, a society revealed itself to the injustice of a totally corrupt and unpunished regime in its institutions that gave justice, fighting for the universal principles of Freedom, Equality, and Fraternity.

Finally, the suggestions described here disagree, of course, from the spirit of "Judicial Reform" that is promoted from the top of the political world by the President of the Supreme Court of Justice Arturo Zaldivar Lelo de la Rea, the Legal Counsel of the Federal Executive Julio Scherer Ibarra and the Senator of the Republic Ricardo Monreal Ávila, because these proposals certainly do not attack the efficient cause of the state problem that this work exhibits.

r. What duty do the attorneys have because of the Justice Administration problem in Mexico?

According to the research, the role and the task of the lawyers, the academy and the law schools, as well as the Bars Associations, throughout the country, was not taken into account to achieve the objectives pretended.

Regardless of this methodological situation, the hypothesis is opened, for further research, that the revealed problem has grieved the Lawyer profession in Mexico, especially to salaries and fees. Likewise, the issue of lawyers salaries is far from the legal regulations in 25 states of Mexico such as public tariffs and representation fees, and this implies that the Access to Justice is impossible for a precarious society such as the Mexican.

In contrast, we argue the rational belief that this problem has caused so much damage, that lawyers, in some cases acquiescent and tolerant to the problem, lend themselves to corrupt and cynical practices that invite society to believe in vengeance as the solution to their problems.

In this regard, the existence of interdependence between the degree of violent homicides for the RICLCRE by the Justice Administration is possible; however, the research does not provide indicators on Public Safety.

It is essential to say that the judges, magistrates, prosecutors, presidents of Boards, public defenders and clerks, all of them, are lawyers, and the manifest and deplorable state in which the Justice Administration in Mexico has become is ethically and professionally unjustifiable, when they are Public Officials responsible for watching over the good standing of their institution.

However, premature judgments should not be made because the problem that this book narrates was not generated a week ago or a month ago, but the research points to a generational and historical problem of at least 50 years of acquiescence to inoperability and the uselessness of the Justice Administration that turned the Courts into Anti-Mexican institutions.

Of course, impunity as a traditional, historical and generational practice of omitting the Justice Administration, possibly suggests the subsistence of lawyers in Mexico and the unworthy form of jurisdictional prosecution.

Therefore, a research that seeks to reveal the alleged associations and possible judicial cartels will pay no further than the necessary and fundamental fact of having published the problem of Public Accountability here exposed, because the vital action is the solution of the issues, not aggravate them.

In a minimal possibility and if the "*Change*" of the Judicial Branches is feasible, What lawyers would "*change*" the new Courts? Would there be Political will to completely change one of the Branches of the Union by democratic means? What guarantee do we have that we will receive justice?

In parochial terms and contrasting the previous approaches, according to the revealed information, the Courts that we have and their authorities represent a Sports Team that fills the stadiums each season with the idyllic dream of raising a trophy, to recreate and delude millions, which is a very bad entertainment industry, expensive and boring at times, but eternally beneficial for some people.

Without Sports comparisons (and many names), in Sports history, it comes the moment of each generation where fans stop going to the stadiums and stop following their teams for lack of " *faith*" in their franchise. As a result, the franchises disappear. Therefore, the franchises are reinvented in each generation since the good of the sport has always lasted, from the Ancient age to the present.

For these reasons, I suggest and consider that an upcoming research will be decisive and definitive about the role of the lawyer into the future, thinking about the role of the lawyer before a reality that at times the propaganda and the illusion of individual factors commands those discussions and deliberations.

Of course, I do not rule out topics related to Artificial Intelligence and an unlikely Legal profession annihilation, but, if Mexico has no fundamental bases that integrate judicial statistics as an instrument of public accountability, Do you think that a machine that was programmed abroad will substitute lawyers without data on the functions, faculties, and competencies of the legal practice?

According to Schrödinger cat's paradox, inside the box, the cat is dead and alive at the same time, and for that reason, one must approach to see how the cat is, no matter if the cat lives or dies, but to appreciate that the box really works to contain the bomb that is inside it, that is next to the cat.

VI. Digital Repository and Bibliography.

a. Petitions and answers from the Federal Government and the 32 states of Mexico are available in the following websites:

- **Federal Government**
  https://www.infomex.org.mx/

- **Aguascalientes**
  http://207.248.118.52/InfomexAgu
  ascalientes/

- **Baja California**
  http://201.140.167.15/InfomexBaja
  California/

- **Baja California Sur**
  http://infomex.bcs.gob.mx/Infomex
  BCS/

- **Campeche**
  http://www.infomex.campeche.gob
  .mx/

- **Chiapas**
  http://sistemas.fpchiapas.gob.mx/p
  ntchiapas/

- **Chihuahua**
  https://transparenciachihuahua.org
  /infomex/

- **Coahuila**
  http://189.254.130.35/infocoahuila/

- **Colima**
  http://www.infomexcolima.org.mx/

- **Mexico City**
  http://www.infomexdf.org.mx/Infom
  exDF/default.aspx

- **Durango**
  http://www.infomexdurango.gob.m
  x/InfomexDurango/

- **State of Mexico**
  https://www.saimex.org.mx/

- **Guanajuato**
  http://www.infomexguanajuato.org.
  mx/infomex/

- **Guerrero**
  http://info.guerrero.gob.mx/

- **Hidalgo**
  https://infomexhidalgo.dyndns.org/
  infomexhidalgo/

- **Jalisco**
  https://www.infomexjalisco.org.mx/
  InfomexJalisco/

- **Michoacan**
  http://michoacan.infomex.org.mx/

- **Morelos**
  https://infomexmorelos.mx/

- **Nayarit**
  http://www.infomexnayarit.gob.mx/
  infomex/

- **Nuevo León**
  http://nl.infomex.org.mx/

- **Oaxaca**
  http://oaxaca.infomex.org.mx/

- **Puebla**
  http://puebla.infomex.org.mx

- **Queretaro**
  http://queretaro.infomex.org.mx/

- **Quintana Roo**
  http://infomexqroo.org.mx/

- **San Luis Potosí**
  https://www.infomexslp.mx

- **Sinaloa**
  https://www.infomexsinaloa.org.m

- x

- **Sonora**
  http://infomex.sonora.gob.mx/

- **Tabasco**
  http://www.infomextabasco.org.mx
  /v25/

- **Tamaulipas**
  https://www.sisaitamaulipas.org/Si
  saiTamaulipas/

- **Tlaxcala**
  http://www.infomextlaxcala.org.mx
  /

- **Veracruz**
  https://infomexveracruz.org.mx/Inf
  omexVeracruz/default.aspx

- **Yucatan**
  https://infomex.transparenciayucat
  an.org.mx/InfomexYucatan/

- **Zacatecas**
  https://infomexzacatecas.org.mx/I
  nfomex/

To check the public information, each website has a link that says *"Consulta aquí las solicitudes de información y sus respuestas, que han realizado otras personas a través de la Plataforma Nacional de Transparencia, da clic aquí".* Click it, next; the Public Office will be available to search the information required by typing the cell FOLIO the number of the petition, following the platform instructions:

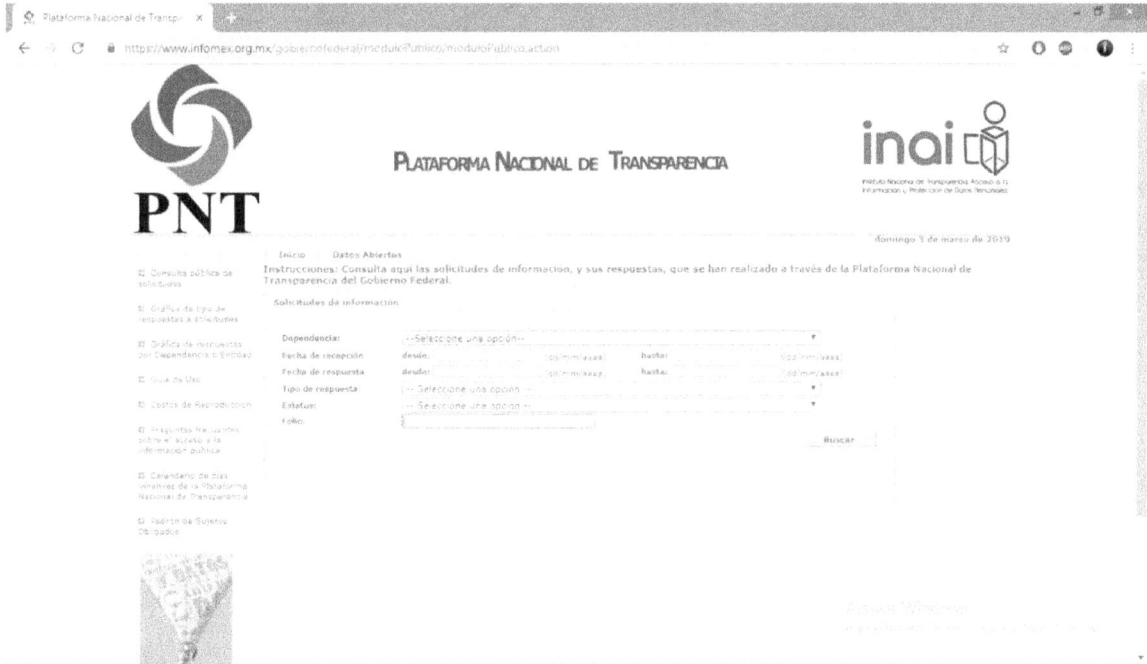

FIGURE 9. Public Office, National Transparency Platform.

b.   Petitions and answers are available in the following Google Drive link.

**https://drive.google.com/drive/folders/1DgHTguVtH2xv3SP1xk4ox6ueSHv
2tViT?usp=sharing**

c.   Bibliography sources (digital) and papers are available in the next links

(*Spanish*)

-   Instituto Nacional de Estadística y Geografía, INEGI.

    o   Censo Nacional de Impartición de Justicia Federal disponible en
        http://www.beta.inegi.org.mx/programas/cnijf/2013/default.html#Tabul
        ados.

    o   Censo Nacional de Impartición de Justicia Estatal 2018, disponible en
        http://www.beta.inegi.org.mx/programas/cnije/2018/   y
        https://www.inegi.org.mx/sistemas/olap/proyectos/bd/censos/gobiern
        o2018/CNIJE2018/ImpJustTM.asp#.

    o   Censo Nacional de Procuración de Justicia Federal 2018, disponible
        en http://www.beta.inegi.org.mx/programas/cnpj/2018/ .

    o   Censo Nacional de Procuración de Justicia Estatal 2018, disponible
        en http://www.beta.inegi.org.mx/programas/cnpje/2018/ .

-   Dirección General de Estadística Judicial del Consejo de la Judicatura Federal.

    o   Estadística judicial del Poder Judicial de la Federación, disponible en
        http://www.dgepj.cjf.gob.mx/paginas/informacionRelevante.htm?page
        Name=informacion%2FanexoEstadisticoWeb.htm

-   Tribunal Federal de Justicia Administrativa.

- o Memoria Anual 2018, disponible en http://www.tfjfa.gob.mx/media/media/memorias/MemoriaAnual2018/index.html.

- Tribunal Federal de Conciliación y Arbitraje.

  - o Informe Mensual de Productividad diciembre 2018; disponible en http://www.tfca.gob.mx/en/TFCA/fraccionXXX.

  - o Estadística judicial desagregada Enero del 2019, disponible en http://tfca.gob.mx/work/models/TFCA/Resource/322/1/images/inform em_enero2019.pdf.

- Tribunal Superior Agrario.

  - o Síntesis estadística a junio del 2018, disponible en http://transparencia.tribunalesagrarios.gob.mx/index.php/component/k2/item/184 .

- Banco de México, BANXICO; *Eficiencia del Sistema de Justicia y Desempeño Económico Regional en México.* Investigación realizada por Juan Carlos Chávez Martín del Campo, Felipe J. Fonseca y Manuel de J. Gómez Zaldivar. Junio de 2017, disponible en http://www.anterior.banxico.org.mx/publicaciones-y-discursos/publicaciones/documentos-de-investigacion/banxico/%7B172DEC87-7CAB-3592-A8A5-1EA2F879DC1F%7D.pdf.

- CONSULTA NACIONAL DE OBLIGACIONES DE TRANSPARENCIA, Instituto Nacional de Transparencia, Acceso a la Información y Protección de Datos Personales, disponible en https://consultapublicamx.inai.org.mx/vut-web/ .

STATE COURTS INFORMATION.

- PODER JUDICIAL DEL ESTADO DE BAJA CALIFORNIA, Estadísticas Judiciales; disponible en http://transparencia.pjbc.gob.mx/paginas/estadisticas.aspx .

- TRIBUNAL SUPERIOR DE JUSTICIA DEL ESTADO DE CHIHUAHUA, Estadísticas Judiciales; disponible en http://www.stj.gob.mx/estadistica/index.php.

- PODER JUDICIAL DEL ESTADO DE COLIMA, Estadísticas judiciales; disponible en https://transparencia.stjcolima.gob.mx/#/declaraciones/56.

- TRIBUNAL DE JUSTICIA ADMINISTRATIVA DEL ESTADO DE DURANGO, información de obligaciones de transparencia, disponible en http://tja.durango.gob.mx/es/Historico2017 y http://tja.durango.gob.mx/es/CuartoTrimestreHistorico2017.

- SUBSECRETARÍA DEL TRABAJO Y PREVISIÓN SOCIAL, Gobierno del Estado de Guanajuato, estadísticas tribunales laborales; disponible en http://sg.guanajuato.gob.mx/sstps/ .

- INSTITUTO DE INFORMACIÓN ESTADÍSTICA Y GEOGRÁFICA DEL ESTADO DE JALISCO; Censo Nacional de Impartición de Justicia Estatal, disponible en https://iieg.gob.mx/contenido/SociedadGobierno/Ficha_imparticion_%20justicia_2018.pdf.

- TRIBUNAL DE JUSTICIA ADMINISTRATIVA DEL ESTADO DE JALISCO, Estadística judicial, disponible en http://portal.tjajal.org/fileman/Uploads/estadi%CC%81stica%202018%20TJAJAL.pdf.

- DATOS ABIERTOS DE LA SECRETARÍA DEL TRABAJO Y PREVISIÓN SOCIAL DEL ESTADO DE JALISCO Y DE LA JUNTA LOCAL DE CONCILIACIÓN Y ARBITRAJE DEL ESTADO DE JALISCO , MIDE LAB, disponible en https://stps.jalisco.gob.mx/justicia-laboral/emplazamientos, y https://seplan.app.jalisco.gob.mx/mide/panelCiudadano/detalleIndicador/359?palabra=laboral&max=10&offset=0&agregado=1&url=buscar&format=.

- TRIBUNAL DE JUSTICIA ADMINISTRATIVA DEL ESTADO DE MICHOACÁN, Estadística judicial, disponible en www.tjamich.gob.mx.

- TRIBUNAL SUPERIOR DE JUSTICIA DEL ESTADO DE MORELOS, Informe de Actividades y Estadística Judicial, disponibles en http://tsjmorelos2.gob.mx/.

- PODER JUDICIAL DEL ESTADO DE NAYARIT, Estadística judicial, disponible en http://www.tsjnay.gob.mx/transparencia/fraccion-xxx-estadisticas/, consúltese anuario estadístico judicial en http://www.tsjnay.gob.mx/wp-content/files/bea/BEA2017.pdf

- PODER JUDICIAL DEL ESTADO DE NUEVO LEÓN, Estadística Judicial; disponible en https://www.pjenl.gob.mx/Estadistica/ .

- MODELO DE EVALUACIÓN Y SEGUIMIENTO DE LA CONSOLIDACIÓN DEL SISTEMA DE JUSTICAI PENAL, disponible en http://www.mes-sjp.com.mx/.

- PODER JUDICIAL DEL ESTADO DE PUEBLA. Estadística judicial, disponible en http://www.htsjpuebla.gob.mx/secciones/estadisticas/.

- TRIBUNAL DE JUSTICIA ADMINISTRATIVA DEL ESTADO DE QUERÉTARO, Estadística judicial, disponible en http://queretarotca.com/tca2/transparencia/estadistica/Juzgados2018.pdf.

- TRIBUNAL SUPERIOR DE JUSTICIA DEL ESTADO DE ZACATECAS, Informes de labores 2000-2018, disponibles en:

  o 2000: http://187.174.173.102:8081/tr/docu/PregFrec/InfAnuales/2000_1erFBE.pdf
  o 2001: http://187.174.173.102:8081/tr/docu/PregFrec/InfAnuales/2001_2doFBE.pdf
  o 2002: http://187.174.173.102:8081/tr/docu/PregFrec/InfAnuales/2002_3erFBE.pdf

- 2003:
  http://187.174.173.102:8081/tr/docu/PregFrec/InfAnuales/2003_4erFBE.pdf
- 2004:
  http://187.174.173.102:8081/tr/docu/PregFrec/InfAnuales/2004_1erBRA.pdf
- 2005:
  http://187.174.173.102:8081/tr/docu/PregFrec/InfAnuales/2005_2doBRA.pdf
- 2006:
  http://187.174.173.102:8081/tr/docu/PregFrec/InfAnuales/2006_3erBRA.pdf
- 2007:
  http://187.174.173.102:8081/tr/docu/PregFrec/InfAnuales/2007_4toBRA.pdf
- 2008: http://187.174.173.102:8081/tr/docu/PregFrec/InfAnuales/2008-1erLVP.pdf
- 2009: http://187.174.173.102:8081/tr/docu/PregFrec/InfAnuales/2009-2doLVP.pdf
- 2010: http://187.174.173.102:8081/tr/docu/PregFrec/InfAnuales/2010-3erLVP.pdf
- 2011: http://187.174.173.102:8081/tr/docu/PregFrec/InfAnuales/2011-4toLVP.pdf
- 2012: http://187.174.173.102:8081/tr/docu/PregFrec/InfAnuales/2012-1erJACR.pdf
- 2013: http://187.174.173.102:8081/tr/docu/PregFrec/InfAnuales/2013-2doJACR.pdf
- 2014: http://187.174.173.102:8081/tr/docu/PregFrec/InfAnuales/2014-3erJACR.pdf
- 2015: http://187.174.173.102:8081/tr/docu/PregFrec/InfAnuales/2015-4toJACR.pdf
- 2016:
  http://187.174.173.102:8081/tr/docu/PregFrec/InfAnuales/2016_1erAAA.pdf
- 2017:
  http://187.174.173.102:8081/tr/docu/PregFrec/InfAnuales/2017_2doAAA.pdf
- 2018:
  http://187.174.173.102:8081/tr/docu/PregFrec/InfAnuales/2018_3erAAA.pdf.

ELECTRONIC INFORMATION.

- ANIMAL POLÍTICO, "Más de 21 mil funcionarios se han amparado contra la Ley de Remuneraciones"; disponible en https://www.animalpolitico.com/2019/01/funcionarios-amparo-ley-remuneraciones/.

- LA SILLA ROTA, "Jueces y Magistrados van contra reducción de salarios; acuden a SCJN, en https://lasillarota.com/jueces-y-magistrados-van-contra-reduccion-de-salarios-acuden-a-scjn/259756.

- DATOS ABIERTOS, Gobierno Federal, consultable en https://datos.gob.mx.

- ESTADÍSTICA DE LA COMISIÓN INTERAMERICANA DE DERECHOS HUMANOS, México, disponible en http://www.oas.org/es/cidh/multimedia/estadisticas/estadisticas.html.

- ESTADÍSTICA DEL COMITÉ DE DERECHOS HUMANOS DE LA ORGANIZACIÓN DE NACIONES UNIDAS; *Statistical Survey on Individual Complaints*, México; disponible en https://www.ohchr.org/en/hrbodies/ccpr/pages/ccprindex.aspx.

- COMUNICADO DE PRENSA, Secretaría de Economía, "México gana arbitraje internacional", disponible en http://www.2006-2012.economia.gob.mx/eventos-noticias/sala-de-prensa/comunicados/5439-mxico-gana-arbitraje-internacional.

- PROCESO, "La derrota de PEMEX ante Siemens le cuesta 500 millones de dólares", disponible en https://www.proceso.com.mx/379209/la-derrota-de-pemex-ante-siemens-le-cuesta-500-millones-de-dolares .

- GOLDSTEIN & RUSSELL, P.C., Representative Clients, disponible en http://www.goldsteinrussell.com/representative-clients/ .

- RECOMENDACIONES INTERNACIONALES A MÉXICO EN MATERIA DE DERECHOS HUMANOS, Secretaría de Relaciones Exteriores, disponible en http://recomendacionesdh.mx/ .

VII.   APPENDIX.

CONSOLIDATED INFORMATION OF PENDING CASES.

2018 PENDING CASES

LABOR LAW AND BUREAUCRATIC LABOR LAW

PENDING CASES

JURISDICTION	LABOR LAW			BUREAUCRATIC LABOR LAW			CONSOLIDATED		
	Before Dec. 31, 1999	Jan. 1, 2000, to Dec. 31, 2010	Jan. 1, 2011,- Act	Before Dec. 31, 1999	Jan. 1, 2000, to Dec. 31, 2010	Jan. 1, 2011,- Act	TOTAL	SUBTOTAL LABOR	SUBTOTAL BUREAUCRATIC
Federal Government	2757	71,979	360,882	48	6348	19,802	461,179	434981	26,198
Guanajuato	159	6100	31784	2	569	4591	43,205	38043	5162
Jalisco	-	-	98000	5	1955	13788	113,748	98000	15748
San Luís Potosi	-	-	-	-	-	-	8,316	8316	
Yucatan	-	-	-	-	-	-	4,442		4442
Morelos	-	-	-	-	-	-	23,703	23703	
Mexico City	197	12629	78808	-	-	-	91,634	91634	
State of Mexico	70	7349	32,015	2	4548	15843	68,925	48,532	20393
Baja California	-	-	-	-	-	-	43,287	43287	
Campeche	93	1698	2511	-	-	-	4,302	4302	
Sinaloa	0	664	5553	0	36	1347	7,600	6217	1383

Aguascalientes	0	656	7288	0	15	1992	9,951	7944	2007
Baja California Sur				0	583	1643	2,226		2226
Coahuila	0	1428	17754	0	5	2026	21,213	19,182	2031
Colima				0	77	3053	3,130		3130
Nuevo Leon	0	13	8608				8,621	8621	
Sonora	4446	13474	25429				43,349	43,349	
Oaxaca				5	20	816	841		841
Tamaulipas	20	487	1366				1,873	1,873	
Veracruz	0	809	9212				10,021	10021	
Zacatecas	0	700	4216	0	0	1954	6,870	4,916	1954
Chihuahua	23	3064	13197				16,284	16,284	
Guerrero							3,000	3,000	
Tlaxcala	17	578	2965	3	493	1192	5,252	3560	1692
Chiapas								16,625	
Durango								6,752	6891
Hidalgo									
Michoacan									
Nayarit									
Puebla									
Queretaro									
Quintana Roo									
Tabasco									

TOTAL	7782	121,628	699,588	65	14649	68047	1,033,240	939,142	94,098
National estimate							1,407,334.72	1,276,576.41	130,758.31
Labor law estimate was calculated by 21 out of 33 jurisdictions; 60.60% revealed.									
Bureaucratic Labor law estimate was calculated by 14 out of 33 jurisdictions; 42.42% revealed.									

PENDING CASES (CIVIL, COMMERCIAL, FAMILY AND CRIMINAL LAW)					
Comparison between INEGI's data and revealed cases					
	CIVIL-COMMERCIAL-FAMILY LAW			CRIMINAL LAW		
Jurisdiction	INEGI 2018	Revealed 2019	Difference	INEGI 2018	Revealed 2019	Difference
Jalisco	0	835,099	835,099	15,167	52,183	37,016
State of Mexico	74,000	406,021	332,021	57,895	-	-
Sonora	41,160	271,330	230,170	3466	10,981	7515
Sinaloa	53	65,128	65,075	1449	-	-
Michoacán	58,263	86,229	27,966	4382	16,572	12190
Coahuila	85,676	91,439	14,220	6552	8457	1905
Aguascalientes	133,804	121,357	-12,447	1274	3975	2,701
Guanajuato	65,600	36,936	-28,664	14945	-	-
Nuevo León	57,216	65,941	8,725	4618	-	-
Tamaulipas	31,705	31,788	83	1547	2157	610
Mexico City	396,310	478,931	82621	17812	-	-
Chiapas	86,294	66,647	-20,247	2,914	4273	1,359
Colima	0	25,180	25,180	0	0	0
Baja California	155,150	276,843	121,693	17312	-	-
Durango	33,116	49,173	31,286	7895	15229	7334
Guerrero	103,316	183,554	80,238	8095	28,386	20291
Quintana Roo	15,004	38,867	23,863	1315	1482	167
Yucatán	13,047	15,514	2467	943	-	-
Zacatecas	33,341	70,000	36659	5312	-	-
Puebla	61,385	454,377	392,992	7441	-	-
TOTAL	1,444,440	3,670,354	2,249,000	180,334	143,695	91,088

National Estimate	5,116,473	National Estimate	200,110.52	
Estimate was formulated by 20 out of 33 available jurisdictions; 60.60% revealed				

ADMINISTRATIVE LAW PENDING CASES		
Jurisdiction	Number	Litigation economic amount charged to the Budget
Federal Court	64,363	$372,115,922,216.38
Aguascalientes	-	-
Baja California	-	-
Baja California Sur	68	$22,865,985.64
Campeche	79	-
Mexico City	20,920	
Chihuahua	-	
Chiapas	911	
Coahuila	144	
Colima	244	
Durango	-	
State of Mexico	4828	
Guerrero	1588	$70,777,299.90
Guanajuato	2188	

Jurisdiction	Number	Amount
Hidalgo		
Jalisco	17947	
Michoacan	1392	
Morelos	-	
Nayarit	602	
Nuevo Leon	-	
Oaxaca	3068	
Puebla	346	$218,854,341.70
Queretaro	1675	-
Quintana Roo	-	
San Luís Potosi	255	
Sinaloa	4252	-
Sonora	7688	
Tabasco	-	
Tamaulipas	198	$23,179,378.19
Tlaxcala		
Veracruz	2126	$345,435,783.79
Yucatan	843	
Zacatecas	242	
TOTAL	135,967	$372,797,035,005.60
National Estimate	147,683.22	$373,934,493,363.56
Estimate was calculated by 30 out of 33 jurisdictions, 90.90% revealed		

Attorney General of the Republic and States Attorney General.						
Temporary file and pending cases						
National Consolidated						
	TCJS			NCJS		
Jurisdiction	Temporary File/ Reserve	Pending	SUBTOTAL	Temporary File/ Reserve	Pending	Subtotal	TOTAL
Aguascalientes	8,626	19,399	28025	19692	23417	43109	71134
Sinaloa	153	26,039	26192	806	29756	30562	56754
Michoacan	270,496	20,167	290,663	94,156	25,624	119,780	410,443
Sonora	26	331	357	247	14,800	15047	15,404
Baja California	306,961	155,975	462936	130,993	137,840	268,833	731,769
Chiapas	-	11,916	11,916	14,247	11,498	25745	37,661
Nuevo Leon	380,769	513,548	894317	0	367,517	367517	1,261,834
Quintana Roo	6,592	88,992	95584	570	13,318	13888	109,472
Yucatán	1,520	173,559	175079	12,127	8519	20646	195725
Zacatecas	1,440	249	1689	5,231	10,062	15293	16982
Veracruz	662	75	737	12195	43483	55678	56415
Oaxaca	12,831	180,276	193107	3136	55472	58608	251715
Durango	9,346	32,378	41724	0	0	0	41724
Guanajuato	0	2	2	58,969	9,034	68003	68005
Jalisco	77,593	18,018	95611	61,985	81,908	143893	239504

TOTAL	1,077,015	1,240,924	2317939	414354	832248	1246602	3564541
National estimate							4,939,420.45
Estimate was calculated by 11 out of 33 jurisdictions, 33.33% revealed.							

Pending cases National consolidated					
Disaggregation					
Jurisdiction	Common/ Criminal Law	Labor Law	Bureaucratic Labor Law	Administrative/ Agrarian Law	AG	TOTAL
Aguascalientes	125,332	7,944	2,007	-	71,134	206,417
Baja California	276,843	43,287	-	-	268,833	588,963
Baja California Sur	-	-	2226	68	-	2,294
Campeche	-	4302	-	79		4,381
Mexico City	485,899	91,634	-	20,920	-	598,453
Chihuahua	-	16,284	-	-	-	16,284
Chiapas	70,920	16,625	-	911	25,745	114,201
Coahuila	99,896	19,182	2031	144	-	121,253
Colima	25,180	-	3,130	244	-	28,554
Durango	64,402	6,752	6,891	-	41,724	119,769
State of Mexico	406,021	48,532	20393	4,828	-	479,774
Guerrero	211,880	3483	-	1588	-	216,951
Guanajuato	36,936	38,043	5,162	2188	68,005	150,334
Hidalgo	-	-	-	-	-	0
Jalisco	887,282	98,000	15,733	17,947	239,504	1,258,466
Michoacan	102,801	-	-	1392	410,443	514,636
Morelos	-	23,703	-	-	-	23,703
Nayarit	36,810	-	-	602	-	37,412

					1,261,834	1,336,396
Nuevo Leon	65,941	8,621	-	-		
Oaxaca	-	-	841	3068	251,715	255,624
Puebla	454,377	-	-	346	-	454,723
Querétaro	-		-	1675	-	1,675
Quintana Roo	40,349	-	-	-	109,472	149,821
San Luís Potosi	-	8316	-	255	-	8,571
Sinaloa	65,128	6,217	1383	4,252	56,754	133,734
Sonora	282,311	43,349	-	7688	15,404	348,752
Tabasco	-	-	-	-	-	0
Tamaulipas	33,945	1,873	-	198	-	36,016
Tlaxcala	-	3,560	1692	-	-	5,252
Veracruz	-	10021	-	2126	56,415	68,562
Yucatan	15,485	-	4442	843	195,725	216,495
Zacatecas	70,000	6870	1954	242	16,982	96,048
Federal Government	464,325	434,981	26,308	114,263	-	1,039,877

HIGH CARD METHOD CONSOLITADED DATA						
JURISDICTION	COURTS	LABOR LAW	BUREAUCRATIC LABOR LAW	ADMINISTRATIVE LAW	CRIMINAL CASES	TOTAL
Aguascalientes	125,332	7,944	2,007	-	71,134	206,417
Baja California	276,843	43,287	-	9579	268,833	598,542
Baja California Sur	1293	-	2226	68	30959	34,546
Campeche	10796	4302	-	79	1621	16,798
MEXICO CITY	512,689	91,634	-	20,920	870,000	1,495,243
Chihuahua	649	16,284	-	-	80,059	96,992
Chiapas	70,920	16,625	-	911	25,745	114,201
Coahuilla	99,896	19,182	2031	144	45188	166,441
Colima	25,180	7578	3,130	244	54277	90,409
Durango	64,402	6,752	6,891	-	41,724	119,769
MEXICO STATE	711,284	48,532	20393	4,828	134243	919,280
Guerrero	211,880	15956	-	1588	53130	282,554
Guanajuato	36,936	38,043	5,162	2188	68,005	150,334
Hidalgo	107121	1604	-	-	120358	229,083
Jalisco	887,282	98,000	15,733	17,947	239,504	1,258,466
Michoacan	102,801	-	-	1392	410,443	514,636
Morelos	68349	23,703	-	-	33618	125,670
Nayarit	36,810	-	-	602	2251	39,663
Nuevo Leon	65,941	8,621	431	2771	1,261,834	1,339,598
Oaxaca	128407	7616	841	3068	251,715	391,647
Puebla	454,377	14874	-	346	88229	557,826
Queretaro	45666	26949	-	1675	18979	93,269
Quintana Roo	40,349	21544	1134	-	109,472	172,499

San Luis Potosi	**17079**	8316	-	255	31534	**57,184**
Sinaloa	65,128	6,217	1383	4,252	56,754	**133,734**
Sonora	282,311	43,349	-	7688	15,404	**348,752**
Tabasco	**24883**	2814	-	-	15360	**43,057**
Tamaulipas	33,945	1,873	-	198	241123	**277,139**
Tlaxcala	**47393**	3,560	1692	-	23642	**76,287**
Veracruz	**255436**	10021	-	2126	56,415	**323,998**
Yucatán	15,485	8846	4442	843	195,725	**225,341**
Zacatecas	70000	6870	1954	242	16,982	**96,048**
FED. GOV. **	464,325	434,981	26,308	114,263	300,000	**1,339,877**
TOTAL	**5,361,188**	**1,045,877**	**95,758**	**198,217**	**5,234,260**	**11,935,300**
Binary 1st edition estimates	5,316,584	1,276,576.41	130,758	147,683	4,939,420.45	12,325,247.70
Difference (+/-)	0.83%	-18.08%	-26.76%	25.49%	5.63%	**-2.58%**
Revealed percentage	*100%*	*90.90%*	*48.49%*	*75.76%*	*100%*	***83%***
Obtained by INEGI data (HIGH CARD)						
WITHOUT NUMBERS DESPITE CLAIMS AND APPEALS.						

List of abbreviations and terminology.

- Average Duration of Resolution of Legal Cases (ADRLC).

- Real Institutional Capacity of Legal Case Resolution (RICLCRE).

- Official Letter (Off.).

- Traditional Criminal Justice System (TCJS).

- New Criminal Justice System (NCJS).

- Transparency Regulator of the State.

- National System/ National Transparency and Public Information System.

- Binary Hidden Scale of Corruption (BHSC).

- Supreme Court of Justice of the Nation (SCJN).

- National Commission of Human Rights (CNDH).

- Legal Counsel of the President of Mexico (CJEF).

- Judiciary Federal Council (CJF).

- Office of the Defense of Labor (PROFEDET).

- Department of State (SEGOB).

- Department of Foreign Affairs (SRE).

- Department of Labor and Social Welfare (STPS).

- Board of Conciliation and Arbitration (JLCA).

- National Institute of Statistics and Geography (INEGI)

- National Institute of Transparency, Access to Information and Personal Data Protection, (INAI).

- National Transparency Platform (PNT).

- Federal Bureaucratic Labor Court (TFCA).

- United Nations Human Rights Council (UNHRC)